THE NATIONAL NOTARY ASSOCIATION

THE U.S. NOTARY LAW PRIMER

A Guide for U.S. States and Territories

National Notary Association

Published by
National Notary Association
9350 De Soto Avenue
Chatsworth, CA 91311-4926
Telephone: (800) 876-6827
Fax: (818) 700-0920
Website: www.NationalNotary.org
Email: nna@NationalNotary.org

The information in this *Primer* is correct and current at the time of its publication, although new laws, regulations and rulings may subsequently affect the validity of certain sections. This information is provided to aid comprehension of state Notary Public requirements and should not be construed as legal advice. Please consult an attorney for inquiries relating to legal matters.

Second Edition ©2014
First Edition ©2012

ISBN: 978-1-59767-137-8

Table of Contents

Tables

Introduction

You are to be commended on your interest in Notary law! Purchasing *The U.S. Notary Law Primer* identifies you as a conscientious professional who takes your official responsibilities seriously.

In few fields is the expression "more to it than meets the eye" truer than in Notary law. What often appears on the surface to be a simple procedure may, in fact, have important legal considerations.

The purpose of *The U.S. Notary Law Primer* is to provide you with a resource to help decipher the notarial laws and practices in your state. This *Primer* is not meant to replace your official state handbook or website for Notaries. Quite the contrary, this *Primer* is meant to be a supplementary resource should your state handbook, website or statutes fail to address a specific topic or situation.

Because state laws vary, this *Primer* is based on industry-recognized professional standards of practice that all Notaries should follow. As a public official, however, you must become familiar with your state's specific statutes, as well as any pertinent official rules and regulations that may supplement statutes. As always, your state laws comprise your primary reference and guide, and should anything presented in this *Primer* contradict those laws, then the laws hold priority.

In this *Primer* you will find the basic Notary Public requirements for all U.S. states and territories. In addition, you will find a thorough discussion of Notary Public best practices to aid you in the many situations you will encounter for which there is no official guidance. For handy reference, we have reprinted the complete text of the guidelines of *The Notary Public Code of Professional*

Responsibility of the National Notary Association, as well as addresses and phone numbers for Bureaus of Vital Statistics, plus a list of nations that are parties to the particular Hague Convention treaty which simplifies the process of authentication of notarized documents exchanged between nations.

Whether you're about to be commissioned for the first time, or are a longtime Notary, we're sure *The U.S. Notary Law Primer* will provide you with new insight and understanding. Your improved comprehension of Notary law will naturally result in your greater competence as a professional Notary Public.

Milton G. Valera
Chairman
National Notary Association

What Is Notarization? Why Is It Important?

Notarization provides authentication that a document is genuine or verification that a statement was made under oath — a vital part of a system that preserves the integrity of important agreements, and ensures the propriety of the documentary transactions that underlie our system of civil and criminal justice.

A Notary Public is an official who is commissioned by a U.S. state or territorial government to serve as an impartial witness to the signing of documents and the administration of oaths.

When the Notary performs his or her duties, individuals, businesses and government agencies may rely on the notarized document as authentic — that its signature is genuine and that its signer acted willingly, intending the terms of the document to be in full force and effect.

Notarization does not guarantee the truth or accuracy of statements in a document. The Notary Public has no obligation to verify a document's contents.

Notarization does not legalize or validate a document. A will or other legal paper that contains invalidating flaws before notarization will contain the same flaws afterward.

A Notary serves in an unbiased manner by:

- Avoiding discrimination or favoritism of any kind.
- Not refusing to perform a notarial act without due cause.
- Not discriminating in the charging or waiving of Notary fees.

Even so, it is not reasonably expected that a Notary must immediately "drop everything" to honor a request for notarization.

Notaries typically have other employment obligations that they must accommodate along with their notarial duties. Some forms of "discrimination" are encouraged, as when a Notary offers free notarizations to senior citizens or military service members. These humanitarian or charitable policies are not considered discriminatory.

As an impartial witness to a transaction, the Notary Public is an effective deterrent to fraud.

To be an impartial witness, the Notary must:

- Not stand to profit or gain from notarizing any document. This includes not only monetary gain, but any other beneficial interest such as gifts or advantages.

- The only gain from a notarization that a Notary is allowed is the state-permitted fee for Notary services. The Notary must not receive fees for notarial acts in excess of those allowed by state law.

- The Notary should decline to notarize in any transaction that would call into question his or her impartiality.

A Notary employee may notarize for any officer, executive, supervisor, coworker, subordinate, client or customer of the employing organization, as long as the Notary will not gain a commission, bonus or other consideration as a result of the notarial act, other than his or her regular wage and/or the statutory Notary fee.

The Notary's Most Important Role

Deterring fraud is the Notary's most important role.

Fraud is any deception causing a person to unknowingly surrender money, property, rights or advantages without appropriate compensation.

The most common fraud involves theft of money or property through forgery, whereby a signature is falsified on a document, which then is used to gain unauthorized or unlawful control of another's money or property.

Through careful identification of document signers, Notaries can detect imposters attempting to execute fraudulent documents that could result in devastating financial losses for innocent persons. The Notary's detailed and accurate notarial journal record can prove that certain fraudulent alterations were later made to a notarized document.

Precautions in completing and attaching notarial certificates actually can prevent such later alterations.

By performing their duties lawfully, expertly and with the highest ethical standards, Notaries can detect and deter imposters and exploitations of vulnerable signers who are being tricked or coerced into executing documents against their own interest. They thereby perform their most valuable function — as impartial witnesses serving the public. ■

10 Most-Asked Questions

Every Notary has a question or two about whether and how to notarize. But certain questions pop up again and again. The following top 10 questions are asked repeatedly at the National Notary Association's seminars, its annual National Conference and through its Notary Hotline.

As with most questions about notarization, the answer is not always a simple "yes" or "no." Rather, the answer sometimes is, "It depends."

1. May I notarize a will?

A Notary should only notarize a will if clear instructions and a notarial certificate are provided. If the signer of the will is relying upon the Notary for advice on how to proceed, the Notary should tell the individual to consult with an attorney. Laws regarding wills differ from state to state. Some states do not require wills to be notarized, while others allow it as one of several witnessing options. Typically, the will itself is not notarized, but accompanying affidavits signed by witnesses are.

The danger in notarizing wills is that would-be testators who have drafted their own wills without legal advice may believe that notarization will make their wills legal and valid. However, even when notarized, such homemade wills may be worthless because the testators failed to obtain the proper number of witnesses, or they omitted important information. In fact, notarization itself may actually void an otherwise properly executed handwritten (holographic) will, because courts have occasionally held that any writing on the document other than the testator's invalidates the will.

2. May I notarize for a stranger with no identification?

Yes. If identification of a signer cannot be based upon identification documents (ID cards), a Notary may rely upon the oath or affirmation of one or more credible identifying witnesses — the exact number depending on state laws and on whether a witness is personally known by the Notary. The ideal credible witness is a reliable individual with no stake in the transaction at hand and with personal knowledge of the signer's identity.

When a credible identifying witness is not available to identify a stranger without IDs, the Notary might have no choice but to decline the request to notarize.

3. May I notarize a photograph?

No. To simply stamp and sign a photograph is improper. A Notary's signature and seal must appear only on a notarial certificate (such as an acknowledgment or jurat) accompanying a written statement signed by another person. However, a signature on a written statement referring to an accompanying or attached photograph may be notarized; if the photograph is large enough, the statement and notarial certificate may even appear on its reverse side. Such formats may be acceptable when notarized photos are requested by persons seeking medical or health licenses, or by legal residents renewing foreign passports. A word of caution here: A Notary should always be suspicious about notarizing a photo-bearing card or document that could be used as a bogus "official" ID.

4. What if there is no room for my seal or if it smears?

Usually, if notarial wording printed on a document leaves no room for a seal, a loose certificate may be attached and filled out instead.

If an initial seal impression is unreadable and there is ample room on the document, another impression may be affixed nearby. The illegibility of the first impression will indicate why a second seal impression was necessary. The Notary should then record in the journal that a second seal was applied.

A Notary should never attempt to fix an imperfect seal impression with pen, ink or correction fluid. That may be viewed as evidence of tampering and cause the document to be rejected by a receiving agency.

5. May I notarize signatures on faxes or photocopies of documents?

Yes. A photocopy may be notarized as long as it bears an original signature, meaning that the photocopy must have been signed by hand. A photocopied signature may never be notarized.

Similarly, a faxed document must be signed in ink if it is to be notarized.

Note that some public recorders might not accept notarized signatures on photocopied or faxed documents because they will not adequately reproduce in microfilming.

6. May I notarize for customers only?

It depends on state law. As a public official, a Notary is not commissioned to serve just the customers or clients of any one business, even when the employer has paid for the bond, commissioning fees and notarial supplies. There is no such officer as a "Notary Private."

In many states, employers may lawfully limit the services of Notary-employees to customers only. It is hardly ever explicitly prohibited by statute — as it is in Arizona — to discriminate between customers and noncustomers in offering or refusing to offer notarial services and in charging or not charging fees. However, this policy is at odds with the principles and practices of *The Notary Public Code of Professional Responsibility*.

Discrimination against anyone who presents a lawful request for notarization is not a suitable policy for a public official commissioned to serve all of the public equally. Also, such discrimination can provide the basis for lawsuits.

Yet, a few states have provisions allowing a Notary and employer to agree to limit the Notary's services to transactions directly related to the employer's business during business hours. This does not permit discrimination between customers and noncustomers, but only between business-related and nonbusiness-related documents.

7. May I notarize a document in a language I cannot read?

Yes. As long as the notarial certificate and document signature are in a language the Notary can read, most Notaries may notarize documents written in languages they cannot read.

However, there are certain difficulties and dangers in doing so. The main difficulty for the Notary is making an accurate journal description of an unreadable document; the main danger to the public and the Notary is that the document may be blatantly fraudulent.

In general it is imprudent for a notarization be performed if the Notary and the principal signer cannot directly communicate in the same language.

8. May I certify a copy of a birth certificate?

No. State laws vary markedly on whether Notaries may certify copies and, if so, what documents may be copy-certified. Notaries in some states are authorized to certify copies only of powers of attorney or of entries in their official journals of notarial acts. Some states do allow Notaries to certify copies, but not copies of documents that are either public records or publicly recordable. Only an officer in a Bureau of Vital Statistics should certify a copy of a birth certificate or other vital public record; a Notary's "certification" of a birth or death record might actually lend credibility to a counterfeit or altered document. Only a recording official should certify a copy of a deed or other recordable instrument.

While certifying copies of vital records is prohibited, a Notary may notarize an affidavit of a person requesting a certified copy of a birth or death certificate.

9. Does a document need to be signed in my presence?

It depends. Documents requiring acknowledgments normally do not need to be signed in the Notary's presence. However, the signer must appear before the Notary at the time of notarization to acknowledge that he or she freely signed for the purposes stated in the document.

An acknowledgment certificate indicates that the signer personally appeared before the Notary, was identified by the Notary and acknowledged to the Notary that the document was freely signed. On the other hand, documents requiring a jurat must always be signed in the Notary's presence, as dictated by the typical jurat wording, "Subscribed (signed) and sworn to before me ..."

A jurat certificate indicates that the signer personally appeared before the Notary, was identified by the Notary, signed in the Notary's presence and was given an oath or affirmation by the Notary.

10. May I notarize for a family member?

It depends. Although many states do not expressly prohibit notarizing for family members, Notaries who do so may violate the statutes prohibiting a direct beneficial interest — especially in notarizing for spouses in states that have community property laws. In addition to the possibility of a financial interest in notarizing for a relative, there might be an emotional interest that can prevent the Notary from acting impartially. For example, a Notary who is asked to notarize a contract signed by his or her brother might attempt to persuade the sibling to sign or not sign. As a sibling, the individual is entitled to exert influence — but this is entirely improper for a Notary.

Even if a Notary has no direct beneficial interest in the document and does not attempt to influence the signer, notarizing for a relative could subject the document to a legal challenge if other parties to the transaction allege that the Notary could not have acted impartially. ■

Tools of the Trade

Notaries need several tools to carry out their duties lawfully and efficiently. Those tools are as important to the Notary as a hammer and saw are to the carpenter. Some of these tools, such as the inking seal, may fulfill specific state requirements. What follows are the recommended tools. As always, you should check your state's requirements for the specifics, such as what must appear — or not appear — in an official seal.

Inking Seal

In all but a few states, the inking seal is the Notary's official seal. Its impression reproduces photographically, a legal requirement. All official notarial acts are authenticated with the seal. It should include the Notary's name, the words "Notary Public," and the jurisdiction of the Notary (name of state or territory). Depending on state or territorial laws, it might also have to include the commission expiration date, the Notary's commission number and the seal manufacturer or vendor identification number. It may also include the state's seal and the name of the county where the Notary's bond is filed.

Seal Embosser

A seal embosser is allowed in many states as an alternative to the inking seal and it is the required official seal in the District of Columbia and the U.S. Virgin Islands. Many states allow Notaries to affix an embossment as a fraud-deterrent supplement to a required inked-seal impression. The seal embosser makes a non-photographically reproducible indentation on the document. Because photocopies of documents can sometimes easily pass as originals today, the embossment can be used to distinguish an original from a photocopy. Also, embossing all pages of a document together can safeguard against the fraudulent substitution or addition of pages.

Journal of Notarial Acts

The Notary's journal provides a record of notarial transactions that may be used as evidence in a court proceeding. It may also protect a Notary from groundless claims of notarial misconduct.

A Notary's journal is required by law in many states, and strongly recommended by state officials in virtually all others. Many states detail specific entries that must be recorded for every notarial act. Others do not.

At a minimum, the NNA recommends that each journal entry include the date, time and type of each official act; the type of document notarized; the signature of each signer; the type of information used to verify the identity of the parties whose signatures were notarized; the fee charged; and, at least for high-value real estate documents, the thumbprint of the signer.

Jurat Stamp

The jurat stamp impresses on an affidavit the jurat wording "Subscribed and sworn to before me this _______ day of ____________, ______ by ___________, proved to me ..." The jurat stamp is more convenient (and safer, since critical wording will not be omitted) than typing the wording on each affidavit that requires it.

Venue Stamp

The venue stamp impresses on the document the phrase, "State of ____________, County of ____________," which indicates where the notarization took place. The venue stamp may be used when otherwise acceptable notarial wording does not contain a venue statement.

Fingerprinting Device

Notaries increasingly are asking signers to affix a thumbprint in the journal. This practice deters imposters who will not want to leave behind such absolute evidence of an attempted fraud and provides proof that the signer actually appeared before the Notary, should this fact later be challenged.

California requires Notaries to obtain a thumbprint for powers of attorney, deeds, quitclaim deeds and deeds of trust affecting any real property. Texas Notaries, however, are forbidden from capturing thumbprints in their journals.

Many Notaries opt for the convenience of an inkless fingerprinting device to act as a fraud deterrent.

Notarial Certificates

When appropriate certificate wording that complies with state requirements is not preprinted on the document, or there is no notarial wording at all for the document, a so-called "loose" certificate may be attached, as long as the document signer is able to find out and indicate to the Notary what type of notarial act is needed.

Preprinted "loose" notarial certificates for acknowledgments, jurats, proofs of execution by subscribing witness and copy certification by document custodian are available.

Errors and Omissions Insurance

Notary errors and omissions insurance provides protection for Notaries who are sued for damages resulting from unintentional notarial mistakes. In the event of a lawsuit, the "E&O" insurance company typically will provide and pay for the Notary's legal counsel and absorb any damages levied by a court or agreed to in a settlement, up to the policy coverage limit. Errors and omissions insurance does not cover the Notary for intentional misconduct. ■

Notary Liability and Managing Risk

For many Notaries, the most intimidating penalty for negligence or misconduct is payment of personal funds as a result of a civil lawsuit. This is understandable. Not only do lawsuits threaten court verdicts or out-of-court settlements that require the Notary to pay for damages, they also impose attorney fees and other legal defense costs for which the Notary is responsible.

A civil lawsuit results when a private person, corporation or other legal entity seeks to recover losses caused by a Notary's alleged misconduct. In a lawsuit, the injured party initiating the suit is called the plaintiff; the party being sued is called the defendant.

A Notary is personally liable for the full amount of damages caused by any misconduct in performing a notarization. Suppose, for example, that a forged and notarized trust deed is used as collateral for a $50,000 home-equity loan. If the lending company cannot find and recover from the imposter who borrowed the money, it likely would sue the Notary for the $50,000. If the Notary had performed the improper notarization during employment, the lending company might also sue the Notary's employer.

The misconduct may be intentional or unintentional, but the Notary may be equally liable. The fact that a mistake was "honest" cannot prevent a lawsuit. For example, if a Notary's failure to affix an official seal results in a deed's rejection by a recorder, causing a real estate transaction to fall through, the sales agent might sue the Notary for the lost sales commission.

There are several ways to manage the risk posed by a Notary's potential misconduct or mistakes. These protections are the Notary bond, errors and omissions insurance, and reasonable care.

The Notary Bond

The potential for a Notary's error or misconduct causing monetary loss is real enough that most states require Notaries to be bonded in order to protect the public. A Notary bond is a guarantee that a person financially damaged by a Notary's misconduct will be reimbursed (up to the limit of the bond) in the event the Notary fails to do so.

Depending on state law, the required Notary bond guarantee ranges from $500 to $25,000. The issuer of the bond is called a surety and is usually a bonding company licensed to do business within the Notary's state. In some states, the surety may be an individual.

How a Bond Functions

It is a common misunderstanding that the bond protects Notaries from civil lawsuits. It does not. The Notary bond protects only the public — those individuals or entities who suffer a financial loss due to a Notary's error or misconduct. The Notary bond does not "insure" the Notary from claims; whatever money is paid out on the Notary's behalf, the Notary is obligated to pay back to the surety.

Suppose a Notary is bonded for $10,000 and sued for $5,000. If the Notary is shown to be liable and cannot pay the $5,000, the bonding company (surety) would pay this amount to the injured party. Then, the bonding company would seek repayment from the Notary. If the Notary did not respond, the bonding company would sue the Notary to recover the $5,000.

If the Notary were found to be liable for $15,000 and could not pay, the Notary would be obligated to the surety for the $10,000 it paid to the injured party and also to the injured party directly for the remaining $5,000.

Errors and Omissions Insurance

There is insurance available for protection against lawsuits targeting a Notary's personal assets. While the bond protects the public, this insurance, called Notary errors and omissions insurance (or E&O insurance), protects the Notary by absorbing the costs of responding to lawsuits resulting from the Notary's unintentional errors, up to the policy's limit. Not only will E&O insurance pay out damages to an injured party after a court verdict or out-of-court settlement, but most policies also will provide attorneys and absorb their fees, along with other defense costs. In a sense, E&O insurance is kind of a "malpractice insurance" for Notaries.

E&O insurance differs from a bond in two major ways. First, unlike the Notary bond that is mandatory in most states, E&O insurance is not required by law; it may be purchased or cancelled by the Notary at any time. Second, although all bond funds paid out by the surety must be paid back by the Notary, the Notary does not reimburse the E&O insurance company for any payments it makes.

Although vulnerability to lawsuits is an occupational hazard of the Notary's office, errors and omissions insurance offers some protection.

Reasonable Care

The Notary's best defense against a lawsuit is use of reasonable care.

Legal definitions of reasonable care vary from state to state, but, in general, it is defined as the degree of attentiveness and precaution that would widely be expected of a person of ordinary prudence and intelligence. The opposite of reasonable care is negligence.

Ordinary Prudence Not 'Average' Practice

If a notarial act results in a lawsuit and the Notary can show that he or she took every precaution that would be expected of a person of ordinary prudence and intelligence, a jury would be strongly compelled to find the Notary blameless. In fact, clear demonstration of reasonable care by the Notary often prevents a lawsuit.

Reasonable care is not necessarily the same care that an average person might take. For example, a Notary accused of identifying a signer based on an informal introduction unsuccessfully argued in court that the average Notary in the local area followed the same unlawful practice (*Transamerica v. Green*, 11 Cal. 3rd 693 89 CR915 1970). It is not enough that the Notary be average. The Notary must be law-abiding. Since an ordinarily prudent person abides by the law, reasonable care means, above all, following whatever notarial duties the law and official instructions may dictate, such as identifying a document signer and affixing an official seal.

Yet, determining exactly how to follow the law, especially a vague law, often is difficult. When the law provides inadequate direction, Notaries should be guided by good business practices and by high standards of honesty and common sense.

One method to ensure that you have followed reasonable care is to perform each notarization following the "Five Steps to Proper Notarization" that are detailed in the next chapter. The recommendations in these steps are from *The Notary Public Code of Professional Responsibility* (republished in its entirety at the back of this book), which constitute a best practices approach to notarization. These recommendations do not replace statute. They are meant to provide guidance on matters that are often not addressed in a particular state's statutes. As always, follow your state guidelines first, particularly if anything in the *Code* conflicts with statute. ■

Five Steps to Proper Notarization

As a Notary Public, you are an official, impartial witness. People depend on your signed and sealed Notary certificates to perform a variety of daily business, legal and personal activities. Your notarizations may be required on everything from a middle school's permission slip for a field trip to a trust deed for purchase of a multi-million dollar condominium unit.

As a Notary, you serve a vital role in your community by protecting your fellow citizens from those bent on stealing money and property through fraudulent documentary transactions. It is sometimes difficult to imagine the importance of the seemingly simple act of completing a certificate and affixing your signature and seal. Yet, history is filled with cases of Notaries who allowed a momentary lapse in their procedure to cause tragic circumstances. For instance, did you know that a Virginia Notary was sentenced to prison after helping two of the 9/11 plane hijackers to fraudulently obtain driver licenses?

The procedures for proper notarization may be accomplished if you continually follow the "Five Steps to Proper Notarization."

You will thereby not only protect the public, but you will also enhance your professional reputation and the reputation of all Notaries Public.

Step One: Require the signer to personally appear at the time of notarization.

Always require personal appearance. Personal appearance means you must see and communicate with the signer face to face, in the same room. None of the other steps can be truthfully completed without the signer physically in front of you. A telephone call, video conference or your recognition of a familiar signature is no substitute for the signer's being in your presence at the time of notarization.

There is no more serious violation by a Notary than failing to require the physical presence of a document signer at the time of notarization. Criminal prosecution, civil lawsuits and administrative penalties against the Notary are only part of the fallout from such an act.

By completing a notarial certificate without the presence of the signer, even the best-intentioned Notary facilitates potential frauds that can inflict financial disaster on unsuspecting victims, especially when the fraud involves real estate.

Sooner or later, almost every Notary will be approached by a trusted friend, relative, client, coworker, supervisor or business associate and asked as a favor to notarize the signature of a third party who is absent.

"My wife is ill and can't come in," the excuse might be. Or, "It would be inconvenient for my husband to come all the way over here just to get this notarized." But when the Notary relinquishes to an unauthorized third party the triple duty of verifying a signer's identity, willingness and awareness, the Notary surrenders control of the notarization.

In a surprisingly high percentage of the cases in which a spouse, business partner or customer has asked a Notary to trust that the signature of an absent spouse or partner is genuine, the signature has proven to be a forgery.

It is an unfortunate reality that the individuals who most often take advantage of Notaries are not strangers with phony IDs, but trusted acquaintances. A vengeful spouse in a crumbling marriage or a disgruntled partner in a dissolving business may have other priorities than keeping faith with a Notary acquaintance — namely, wresting control of valuable property from the spouse or partner using a phony document with a forged signature and then pocketing the assets.

Step Two: Identify the signer and screen for willingness and awareness.

You must properly identify the signer for every notarization. By identifying signers, you deter imposter's intent on forgery. In addition, you should ensure that the individual is willingly engaging in the transaction, and that this person seems to be aware of the document's contents.

The Notary establishes the identity of a document signer

through personal knowledge of the signer or through satisfactory evidence. (See "Identifying Document Signers," pages 51–63.)

Step Three: Review the document for completeness and any obvious frauds.

As a Notary you must scan a document's text to verify that the document appears complete and to extract data for your journal entry.

Documents that are not complete or have blank spaces may not be notarized.

Blank spaces on a document are an invitation to fraud. For instance, a promissory note that is incomplete, may later be filled in with a higher interest rate than what was agreed to by the borrower and the lender.

As a prudent Notary you should refuse such notarizations and in some states refusing to notarize a blank or incomplete document is a requirement of law. You may tell the signer the blanks must be completed or lined through. The signer may write "N/A" or "Not Applicable" in the blank, and this late insertion might be noted in your Notary journal under the "Additional Information" column.

Acceptable Blanks. On rare occasions there are acceptable reasons for leaving a space blank, for instance a paper requiring more than one signature may have the "Date of Signing" left blank until the final signature is obtained.

In addition, a recordable document should not be regarded as incomplete because the box labeled "Reserved for Use by Recorder" has not been filled in.

Step Four: Complete the journal entry. (Journals are required in some states, but strongly recommended in all states.)

A journal of notarial acts is a detailed, chronological record of the Notary Public's official acts. The Notary's journal can provide valuable evidence in the event a notarized document is lost or altered, or if certain facts about the transaction are challenged. Your journal helps protect the public's rights to property and to fair treatment under the law. In addition, it can help you defend yourself should you be falsely accused of wrongdoing.

While many states require Notaries to keep a journal, some do not. Nevertheless, every Notary should keep a record book of notarial acts, whether required by law or not. It is simply the prudent, commonsense thing to do and a sound business practice. (See "Journal of Notarial Acts," pages 64–65.)

Step Five: Complete, sign and affix the official seal to the certificate.

The fifth step is to complete the notary certificate. This involves filling in wording, signing with your official signature, and affixing your seal.

The notary certificate outlines the facts you have certified in performing the notarization. It's your official statement of what you have verified.

Many states have laws that stipulate specific certificate wording for each type of notarial act. Other states prescribe no wording at all and allow for a range of certificate formats. (See "Notary Certificate," pages 65–68 and "Notary Seal," page 68.)

As you can see, these Five Steps to Proper Notarization are simple to follow, and cover the most important responsibilities you have as a Notary. Commit them to memory and practice them and soon they will become second nature.

Once again …

Five Steps to Proper Notarization

1. Require the signer to personally appear at the time of notarization.

2. Identify the signer and screen for willingness and awareness.

3. Review the document for completeness and any obvious frauds.

4. Complete the journal entry. (Journals are required in some states, but strongly recommended in all states.)

5. Complete, sign and affix the official seal to the certificate. ■

Notary Laws and Best Practices Explained

In layperson's language, this chapter discusses and clarifies some of the important laws and best practices that guide Notaries Public in the performance of their duties. Many of the individual state law requirements will be found in tables organized in pertinent categories. The best practices will be found in *The Notary Public Code of Professional Responsibility* reprinted in its entirety beginning on page 96.

THE NOTARY COMMISSION

Qualifications for Notary Commission

To become a Notary Public, obtain an application and instructions from your Notary Public Regulator. A complete list of these authorities may be found beginning on page 129.

The following table lists some of the special qualifications for a Notary Public commission in all U.S. states and territories. The information in this table is effective for applications filed on or after January 1, 2012.

Age. In general, all states and territorial jurisdictions require an applicant to be 18 years or older, except for Nebraska (19), Puerto Rico (21) and the U.S. Virgin Islands (21).

Residency. All states require applicants to reside in the state issuing the Notary commission, though some additionally permit residents of nearby states to apply, as long as they work or conduct business in the state issuing the commission. Wisconsin is unique in allowing any resident of any state to qualify for a Notary commission.

English Proficiency. Recognizing the need for clear communication, many states stipulate that Notaries have the ability to read and write in English.

Citizenship. Several states explicitly require U.S. citizenship or legal residency for becoming a Notary Public. Any requirement of U.S citizenship alone is no longer enforced, due to a 1984 U.S. Supreme Court decision, *Bernal v. Fainter*, prohibiting states from making U.S. citizenship a requirement for a Notary commission.

Background Checks. Many states require that applicants for a Notary Public commission be free of convictions of crimes involving dishonesty or moral turpitude. These are spelled out in the tables, with some states requiring applicants to have had their civil rights restored or to be free of convictions for 5 to 10 years prior to applying. California requires applicants to be fingerprinted to enable background checks.

Table 1 — Qualifications for Notary Commission

State	Special Requirements	Course/Test
AK	No felony convictions in 10 years	Recommended by state
AL	Approval by county probate judge required	At discretion of county probate judge
Am. Samoa	Have regular place of work in Am. Samoa; read/write English; submit fingerprints	1st-timers or renewals to pass approved 3-hr. course
AR	U.S. citizen or perm. resident alien; legal resident of AR or adjoining state employed in AR; read/write English; no commission revoked in 10 years	None
AZ*	Read/write English; no felony conviction unless civil rights restored; no AZ commission revoked; U.S. citizen or perm. resident alien	Keep approved manual of duties and responsibilities

Table 1 — Qualifications for Notary Commission		
State	**Special Requirements**	**Course/Test**
CA*	Pass background check including fingerprints; temporary Notary commission for those non-compliant with child or family support orders; military base Notaries need not be residents	1st-timers 6-hr. course; renewals 3-hr.; proctored test
CO*	Read/write English; no misdemeanor involving dishonesty in 5 years; no felony convictions; no Notary commission revoked	1st-timer or renewal expired more than 30 days need class and exam
CT	Non-resident okay w/principal place of business in CT; no felony or other crime involving dishonesty, moral turpitude; no previous commission revoked; no past notarial misconduct	Written exam on application form
DC	Non-resident must work in DC	Oral training/exam session
DE	Non-resident okay w/DE workplace; reasonable need for commission; good character and reputation; no felony convictions of crimes involving dishonesty, moral turpitude; certain residents of any state qualify to notarize electronically	None
FL*	Had civil rights restored if ever convicted of felony	1st-timer takes 3-hr. state-approved course
GA*	Non-resident regularly employed/carrying out business in county of application; read/write English; have/provide operating telephone number	None required. Online course available at http://training.gscca.org
Guam	Read/write English	1st-timer pass a written 45-minute exam
HI*	U.S. citizen, national or perm. resident alien authorized to work in U.S.; read/write English; no drug dependence	Written, closed-book exam
IA	Non-resident from bordering state okay w/place of business in IA; no felony conviction or adjudged mental incompetence	None

Table 1 — Qualifications for Notary Commission		
State	**Special Requirements**	**Course/Test**
ID	Read/write English; non-resident employed in ID qualifies; never removed from office for misconduct/convicted of serious crime in 10 years.	None
IL*	Resident for at least 30 days; non-resident from bordering state employed in IL may qualify; U.S. citizen or perm. res. alien; read/write English; no felony convictions; no Notary commission revoked or suspended in 10 years	None
IN	Not hold lucrative public office in U.S. or IN gov.; no conviction of crime w/sentence exceeding 6 months imprisonment	None
KS	Resident of bordering state okay if regularly employed in or w/ business in KS; no felony convictions or licenses revoked	None. Course required for Electronic Notaries
KY	Non-resident okay if employed in KY county of application; for Special Commission, applicant needn't reside or work in KY; no felony convictions unless civil rights restored	None
LA	Read/write English; citizen or lawfully residing alien; not be "under interdiction or incapable of serving as a notary because of mental infirmity"	Statewide Notary exam for non-attorneys
MA*	Non-resident okay if conduct business on regular basis in MA	None
MD	Non-resident okay if work in MD; of good character, integrity and abilities	None

Table 1 — Qualifications for Notary Commission

State	Special Requirements	Course/Test
ME	Adjacent state resident okay if employed or in business in ME; proficient in English; no commission revocation in 5 years; no convictions punishable by imprisonment for 1 year or more, or offense incompatible with Notary duties in 10 years	Open-book exam on application
MI*	Non-resident okay if maintain place of business in MI; read/write English; no felony convictions in 10 years; not currently imprisoned; no conviction for 2 or more misdemeanors of Notary Act in 12 mos. or 3 or more in 5 yrs.	None, but obtain and read copy of all current statutes regulating notarial acts
MN*	Non-residents okay if from IA, ND, SD or WI	None
MO*	Registered voter or U.S. perm. res. alien; reside in county of application; non-resident okay if employed in MO; read/write English; no commission revoked in 10 years	Computer-based or other training approved by Sec. of State
MS*	Reside in MS at least 30 days; read/write English; U.S. citizen or perm. res. alien; no felony conviction unless pardoned or voting rights restored; not incarcerated, on probation or parole	None
MT*	Reside in MT at least 30 days; no felony conviction; no Notary commission revoked in any state	1st-timers or renewals expired more than 30 days must take training
NC*	Min. 18 yrs. or legally emancipated; non-resident okay w/ regular place of work in NC; speak/read/write English; high school diploma or equivalent; purchase and keep most recent manual approved by Sec. of State on Notary duties	1st-timers 6-hr. course; 1st-timers and renewals pass written exam; attorneys exempt.

Table 1 — Qualifications for Notary Commission		
State	**Special Requirements**	**Course/Test**
ND	Non-resident okay if place of employment in ND or residing in county bordering ND in reciprocating state; read/write English	None
NE*	Min. 19 years old; read/write English; no conviction for crime of fraud or dishonesty.	1st-timer and renewal w/ expired comm. to pass open-book, "take-home" exam
NH*	Be endorsed by 2 NH Notaries and 1 registered voter	None
NJ*	Non-resident of adjoining state okay if employed in NJ; no convictions for crime of dishonesty, or of 1st or 2nd degree	None
NM*	Read/write English; no guilty or *nolo contendere* plea to felony, or conviction; no Notary commission revoked in 5 years	None
N. Mariana Islands	Any U.S. citizen okay if resident of Islands and employed by U.S. gov. or by contractor working for U.S. gov.	None
NV*	U.S. citizen or perm. res. alien; non-residents of bordering states may apply; if felon, civil rights restored	1st-timer and renewal if expired 1 year or fined for violating Notary law; 4-hr. course
NY*	Non-resident okay w/ place of business in NY; U.S. citizen or perm. res. alien; good moral character; equivalent of "common school education"; no felony or certain misdemeanor convictions, unless pardoned or parole board good conduct certified	Proctored, closed-book, 1-hour exam
OH*	Non-resident attorney okay if licensed to practice and with office in OH; each county oversees application process, w/ local bar assn. often involved; local judge must endorse	None unless dictated by local county

Table 1 — Qualifications for Notary Commission		
State	**Special Requirements**	**Course/Test**
OK	Non-resident okay if employed in OK; no felony convictions	None
OR*	Non-resident okay if from adjacent state and employed in OR; read/write English; good moral character; no Notary commission revoked in 5 yrs.; no felony or lesser offense convictions incompatible with duties of Notary in 10 yrs.	1st-timers and expired renewals take 3-hr. course
PA*	Non-resident okay if employed in PA; of good character, integrity and ability; no convictions or pleas of guilt or *nolo contendere* to felony or lesser offense incompatible with duties of Notary in 5 yrs.; no Notary commission revoked in 5 yrs.	1st-timers and all renewals take 3-hr. course
P. Rico	Only attorneys of good moral character, over 21 yrs. of age and designated by Supreme Ct. of Puerto Rico may practice as Notaries	Notarial law exam required
RI*	Be registered voter in RI or atty. who is member of RI bar	None
SC	Applicant must be registered voter in SC	None
SD	Non-resident okay if from county bordering SD and working in state; no felony convictions	None
TN*	Non-resident okay w/principal place of business in TN; U.S. citizen or perm. res. alien; no convictions of bribery/larceny/certain other offenses unless restored to citizenship; no member of U.S. military or holder of office for other state or fed. gov.	None
TX*	No convictions for felony/crime of moral turpitude; escrow agents who are residents of state adjacent to TX may qualify	None

Table 1 — Qualifications for Notary Commission

State	Special Requirements	Course/Test
UT*	Resident at least 30 days; non-resident okay with perm. resident status; read/write/speak/understand English	Online open-book test
VA*	Read/write English; no felony convictions unless pardoned, had rights restored or had conviction vacated	None
Virgin Islands, U.S.	Min. 21 years old; USVI resident for 5 years, except for attorneys; U.S. citizenship; accredited high school graduate or passed equivalency exam; no convictions for any crime	None
VT	Superior Court judges have authority to appoint Notaries.	None
WA*	Non-resident from OR or ID okay if regularly employed in WA; read/write English	None
WI	At least 8th grade education; no felony/misdemeanor convictions involving public trust unless pardoned; WI residency not required, but all acts must be done in state	None, but free online tutorial recommended to prove familiarity w/law
WV	Non-resident okay if works in WV; not disqualified from voter registration due to felony conviction; read/write English; no Notary commission revoked in 10 years	None
WY	Read/write English; no felony convictions unless reversed, annulled, pardoned or rights restored	None

* A complete *Notary Law Primer* is published for this state by the National Notary Association. Each such *Primer* is devoted exclusively to an in-depth examination of the statutes, regulations, rulings, directives and customs governing Notaries in the one state.

Term, Jurisdiction and Bond

The term of office, jurisdiction and bonding of Notaries vary from state to state. Most states set a four-year term of office, but terms do range from two years to life. Most states limit Notaries to acting within their geographic borders. And bonding requirements vary from $500 to $25,000.

The following table lists the term of office, jurisdiction and Notary bond requirements for all U.S. states and territories. The information in this table is effective for commissions issued on or after January 1, 2012.

Table 2 — Term, Jurisdiction and Bond

State	Term of Office	Jurisdiction	Bond
AK	4 years	Statewide	$1,000
AL	4 years	Statewide	$25,000
Am. Samoa	2 years	All AS islands, waters	$500
AR	10 years	Statewide	$7,500
AZ*	4 years	Statewide	$5,000
CA*	4 years	Statewide	$15,000
CO*	4 years	Statewide	Not required
CT	5 years	Statewide	Not required
DC	5 years	District-wide	$2,000
DE	1st term 2 years; renew 2 or 4 years	Statewide	Not required
FL*	4 years	Statewide	$7,500
GA*	4 years	Statewide	Not required
Guam	4 years	Island-wide	$1,000
HI*	4 years	Statewide	$1,000
IA	3 years resident; 1 year non-resident	Statewide	Not required
ID	6 years	Statewide; outside state for deeds filed in Idaho	$10,000
IL*	4 years resident; 1 year non-resident	Statewide	$5,000
IN	8 years	Statewide	$5,000
KS	4 years	Statewide	$7,500

Table 2 — Term, Jurisdiction and Bond			
State	**Term of Office**	**Jurisdiction**	**Bond**
KY	4 years	Statewide; outside state for qualified Notaries if docs. recorded in KY	Varies by county
LA	Life	Statewide for attorneys; parishwide for non-attorneys unless pass exam	$10,000 for non-attorneys and ex officios
MA	7 years	Statewide	Not required
MD	4 years	Statewide	Not required
ME	7 years resident; 4 years non-resident	Statewide	Not required
MI*	6-7 years depending on birthday	Statewide	$10,000
MN*	5 years (expires Jan. 31 in 5th yr.)	Statewide	Not required
MO*	4 years	Statewide	$10,000
MS*	4 years	Statewide	$5,000
MT*	4 years	Statewide with neighbor state reciprocity possible	$10,000
NC*	5 years	Statewide	Not required
ND	6 years	Statewide with neighbor state reciprocity possible	$7,500
NE*	4 years	Statewide	$15,000
NH*	5 years	Statewide	Not required
NJ*	5 years	Statewide	Not required
NM*	4 years	Statewide	$10,000
N. Mar. Islands	2 years	All CNMI islands, waters	$1,000
NV*	4 years	Statewide	$10,000
NY*	4 years	Statewide	Not required
OH*	5 years	Statewide	Not required
OK	4 years	Statewide	$1,000
OR*	4 years	Statewide	Not required
PA*	4 years	Statewide	$10,000

Table 2 — Term, Jurisdiction and Bond			
State	**Term of Office**	**Jurisdiction**	**Bond**
P. Rico	Life	Puerto Rico	$15,000
RI*	4 years	Statewide	Not required
SC	10 years	Statewide	Not required
SD	6 years	Statewide	$5,000
TN*	4 years	Statewide	$10,000
TX*	4 years	Statewide	$10,000
UT*	4 years	Statewide	$5,000
VA*	4 years	Statewide; outside state for docs used in VA or by U.S. gov.	Not required
Virgin Islands, U.S.	4 years	All USVI islands, waters	$10,000
VT	4 years (expires Feb. 10 in 4th yr.)	Statewide; outside state for docs. recorded in VT	Not required
WA*	4 years	Statewide	$10,000
WI	4 years	Statewide	$500
WV	10 years	Statewide	Not required
WY	4 years	Statewide with neighbor state reciprocity possible	$500

* A complete *Notary Law Primer* is published for this state by the National Notary Association. Each such *Primer* is devoted exclusively to an in-depth examination of the statutes, regulations, rulings, directives and customs governing Notaries in the one state.

COMMON NOTARIAL ACTS

The most common notarial acts that are permitted in all states are:

- Acknowledgments
- Oaths and affirmations
- Jurats (also known as verifications upon oath or affirmation)

Depending on state law, you may, or may not, be permitted to perform some of the following acts:

- Copy certification
- Proof of execution by subscribing witness
- Signature witnessing
- Deposition
- Protest
- Marriage ceremony
- Witness opening of safe deposit box

Acknowledgments

Purpose. An acknowledgment is perhaps the most widely performed notarial act. The acknowledgment may be needed with a variety of important documents such as deeds, powers of attorney and loan agreements. The main purposes of an acknowledgment are positive identification of the document signer and verification that the signer freely signed the document.

As long as the signer acknowledges freely signing the document, the Notary does not have to witness the actual signing.

An acknowledgment requires you to certify three facts:

1. Personal Appearance: The signer personally appeared before you at the time of the act.

2. Positive Identification: You positively identified the signer as the person he or she claims to be.

3. Acknowledgment of Signature: The signer must "acknowledge" to you that he or she freely signed the document. The signer may without duress sign the document in front of you, which proves this fact. However, if the document has already been signed, the signer must declare to you to have freely made the signature.

Additionally, many acknowledgment certificates require the certification of other facts by the Notary. For example, determining the authority of the signer to act in a claimed representative capacity is a requirement in many states. Some states even require signers to take an oath or affirmation vouching that they have authority to sign on behalf of a legal entity such as a corporation.

The Notary is obligated to verify any claims made in the Notary certificate. For instance, if the certificate states that the signer is "known to be the president of XYZ Corporation," you must know that this is true. Careful reading of the Notary certificate will reveal any facts that you need to verify.

Acknowledgment Certificates. Acknowledgment certificate wording can vary greatly from state to state, but generally all wording indicates the three facts certified by the Notary: 1) the signer's personal appearance before the Notary, 2) identification of the signer by the Notary, and 3) the signer's acknowledgment to the Notary.

Following is a typical acknowledgment certificate:

State of ______________)
) SS.
County of _____________)

On this ______ day of ______ (month), ______ (year), before me, ____________ (name of Notary), the undersigned Notary Public, personally appeared ____________ (name[s] of signer[s]), personally known to me (or proved to me on the basis of satisfactory evidence) to be the person(s) whose name(s) is/are subscribed to the within instrument and acknowledged that he/she/they freely executed it.

Witness my hand and official seal.

____________ (signature and seal of Notary)

Certificate Wording Prescribed by State Law. Many states prescribe specific wording for common acknowledgment certificates, and Notaries must use only certificate wording that substantially complies with these formats. Some states prescribe no certificate formats at all and allow a wide range of wordings to be used. Notaries must be keenly aware of their state's requirements.

Oaths and Affirmations

Purpose. An oath is a solemn, spoken pledge to a Supreme Being while an affirmation is a solemn, spoken pledge on one's own personal honor. Simply put, oaths and affirmations are spoken promises of truthfulness or loyalty, and both achieve the same legal result.

Oaths and affirmations may be administered as part of a notarial act (such as with a jurat, explained later in this chapter). They may be administered in conjunction with notarizing a document (such as when swearing in a credible identifying witness); or they may stand on their own as a notarial act. An oath of office, for example, is a full-fledged notarial act in its own right when administered by a Notary, even when there is no document or certificate. Most often, Notaries will administer oaths or affirmations as part of the execution of a jurat or when swearing in a credible identifying or a subscribing witness.

Wording for Oaths and Affirmations. State laws and regulations do not always prescribe exact wording for a particular oath or affirmation. And the oath- or affirmation-taker may or may not furnish the Notary with the necessary wording. If there is no wording provided in a given instance, the following examples may be acceptable.

Jurat oath or affirmation:

OATH: Do you solemnly swear that the statements in this document are true, so help you God?

AFFIRMATION: Do you solemnly affirm that the statements in this document are true?

Credible identifying witness oath or affirmation:

OATH: Do you solemnly swear that you know the signer truly holds the identity he (or she) claims, so help you God?

AFFIRMATION: Do you solemnly affirm that you know the signer truly holds the identity he (or she) claims?

Response Required. The oath or affirmation wording must be spoken aloud, and the person taking the oath or affirmation must either repeat the wording spoken by the Notary or answer affirmatively with, "I do," "Yes," or the like. A nod or grunt is not a clear and sufficient response. If a person is mute and unable to speak, the Notary may rely on written notes to communicate.

Ceremony and Gestures. To impress upon the oath- or affirmation-taker the importance of truthfulness, the Notary should lend a sense of ceremony and formality to the oath or affirmation. Some states recommend that the person swearing or affirming raise his or her right hand during the ceremony.

Certificate. When the oath or affirmation is not associated with another notarial act (such as with a jurat or swearing in a credible identifying witness), there may be no document or notarial certificate involved. Oaths and affirmations may qualify as notarial acts even without a document or certificate.

Journal Entry. There should always be an entry in the Notary's journal to record an oath or affirmation given as a notarial act by itself. The entry should include the date and time the oath or affirmation was administered, the type of oath or affirmation (e.g., "mayor's oath of office"), the name and address of the oath-taker or affirmant, how the individual was identified, any fee charged and the signature of the oath-taker or affirmant.

Jurats or Verifications Upon Oath or Affirmation

Purpose. Like the acknowledgment, the jurat, or verification upon oath or affirmation, is one of the most common notarial acts. A jurat requires an individual to sign a document in the presence of the Notary and take an oath or affirmation attesting to the truthfulness of the contents of the document.

Jurats are customarily executed on documents such as affidavits and depositions, which may be submitted as evidence in trials and other official proceedings.

A jurat or verification requires that you certify four facts:

1. Personal appearance: The signer appeared in person before you.

2. Witnessing of signature: You must watch the signer sign. If the document has already been signed, instruct the signer to sign again.

3. Administer an oath or affirmation.

4. Positive Identification: You positively identified the signer as the person he or she claims to be. While positive identification of the signer may not be an express requirement of law for jurats in some states, it is a best practice policy that the NNA strongly encourages.

You must administer the oath or affirmation and the signer thereby declares the statements in the document are truthful and accurate. You do not need to verify personally that the document statements are truthful, but you must have the signer declare it.

Certificate Wording. In executing a jurat, the Notary must complete a notarial certificate that is either contained within or attached to the signed document. The jurat wording is typically far simpler than the wording for an acknowledgment.

The jurat certificate describes the facts that the notarial act certifies: 1) the signer's personal appearance before the Notary, 2) the signature affixation being witnessed by the Notary, 3) the signer's taking of an oath or affirmation, and 4) in some states, the Notary's positive identification of the signer.

Following is an example of typical jurat wording:

State of ________________)
) SS.
County of ______________)

Subscribed and sworn to (or affirmed) before me this ______day of ______ (month), ______ (year), by _____________ (name of signer).

_____________ (signature and seal of Notary)

The actual wording of jurat certificates can vary considerably from one document to the next and from one state to another. For affidavits, the jurat certificate often will be divided into two parts, with the venue appearing at the beginning of the document, the jurat wording (the statement of particulars plus the signature and seal of the Notary) at the end, and the document's text and affiant's signature in between. (The signer of an affidavit is called the affiant.)

Copy Certifications

Purpose. The purpose of this notarial act is to create a copy and certify that it is a true, complete and correct reproduction of the original document. State law may prohibit copy certifications by a Notary of some or all documents.

Certificate Wording. The following is an example of a notarial certificate for a certified copy of an original document presented to a Notary:

State of ________________)
) SS.
County of ______________)

On this ______ day of ______ (month), ______ (year), I certify that the attached or preceding document of ______ (number of pages) pages is a true, exact, complete and unaltered photocopy of _____________ (name or description of original document), presented to me by _____________ (name of original document's custodian), and that, to the best of my knowledge, the original document is neither a public record nor a publicly recordable instrument.

_____________ (signature and seal of Notary)

Not for Vital Records. If your state law permits copy certification, you may not certify copies of original vital records such as a birth or death certificates, or a publicly recordable document such as a deed. Copies of these documents may lawfully be certified only by officials in the relevant public record office.

Alternative. In states that do not authorize Notaries to certify copies, Notaries may notarize a signed, written declaration made by the owner or holder of a document that a copy is a true copy of the original. This process is commonly called "copy certification by document custodian" and may serve as an acceptable alternative to a Notary-certified copy. The receiving party determines if this alternative is acceptable. The requesting person, not the Notary, should provide the declaration and specify the notarial act to be performed if a notarial certificate is not already provided on the declaration. Notaries should be careful not to guide the process or to make any recommendations or claims concerning the legality or sufficiency of this alternative.

Proofs of Execution of Subscribing Witness

Definition. A proof of execution is a notarial act that is performed when the document signer is unable to personally appear before the Notary. A "proof" is then often acceptable under law in place of an acknowledgment — but not in every case.

Procedure. Proofs of execution are used when the principal signer is out of town or otherwise unavailable to appear before a Notary. The steps for performing a proof are:

- The signer (principal) directs a disinterested person (the subscribing witness) to witness his or her signing of a document (or the signer may acknowledge to the subscribing witness that he or she signed the document in their absence).

- The principal directs the subscribing witness to sign the document and then take the document to a Notary in order to "prove" the authenticity of the principal's signature and the fact that it was made willingly.

- The Notary administers an oath or affirmation to the subscribing witness, who must swear or affirm that the principal's signature is genuine and willing and that he or she (the subscribing witness) was requested to sign the document as a witness and take it to a Notary.

Because of the high potential for fraud, proofs of execution are prohibited in many states and restricted in others. For instance, only Notaries who are also members of the bar association may perform a proof in Pennsylvania. Consult your state's laws before attempting to perform this act.

Certificate Wording. The following is an example of a certificate for a proof of execution by subscribing witness:

State of ________________)

) SS.

County of ______________)

Before me, _____________ (name of Notary), on this day personally appeared _____________ (name of subscribing witness), personally known to me (or proved to me on the oath of _____________ [name of person identifying the subscribing witness]) to be the person whose name is subscribed as a witness to the foregoing instrument, and who, after being duly sworn (or affirmed) by me, stated on oath (affirmation) that he/she saw _____________ (name of principal signer), the person who executed the foregoing instrument, subscribe the same (or acknowledge in his/her presence having executed the same) for the purposes and considerations therein expressed, and that he/she had signed the same as a witness at the request of the person who executed the same.

Given under my hand and seal of office this ______ day of ______ (month), ______ (year).

_____________ (signature and seal of Notary)

Signature Witnessings

Definition. The simplest of all of acts, some states allow a Notary merely to certify that that the signer was identified and signed the document in his or her presence

Depositions

Definition. A deposition is a signed and sworn transcript of a person's oral statements for use in a lawsuit or trial. Many states technically authorize Notaries to take depositions, but because creating a written transcript from spoken testimony requires special skills, this is usually left to a trained stenographer or court reporter who is also a Notary or has oath-administering authority.

Notaries without specialized training should not attempt to take depositions — though any Notary may swear in a deponent prior to giving testimony, or execute a jurat on an already created deposition.

Certificate Wording. Deposition certificates and their jurats often require highly specialized language and formatting, depending upon the rules of the jurisdiction or court in which they will be filed — another reason why only Notaries with specialized training should attempt depositions.

Protests

Definition. A protest is a written statement by a Notary or other authorized officer indicating that payment for a negotiable instrument has not been received. Special knowledge of financial and legal terms and procedures is required to perform this notarial act.

Notaries should execute a protest only if they have proper training or if they do so under the supervision of an experienced bank officer or attorney — a requirement that California has placed in statute.

Marriages

In Florida, Maine, Nevada and South Carolina, Notaries have the authority to perform marriages. In all other states, the Notary Public may not "solemnize nuptials" unless the Notary is also a member of the clergy.

Witnessing Safe Deposit Box Opening

Purpose. In many states law permits financial institutions, such as banks, to open a safe-deposit box if the rental fees are overdue, attempts have been made to notify the renter and no response has been received.

Procedure. If the rental fee on a safe deposit box has not been paid, and the financial institution has given proper notice to the lessee, an employee of the financial institution may open the safe deposit box in the presence of a Notary Public. The Notary will usually witness the opening of the box, inventory its contents and complete a certificate certifying such. The certificate is then mailed to the lessee's last known address. If the Notary keeps a journal of notarial acts, it is recommended that the Notary obtain the signatures of the officer of the financial institution and any other witnesses involved in the act. Laws pertaining to the opening of a safe deposit box vary by state.

The following table lists the authorized acts and maximum notarial fees permitted for each of the states and territories.

Table 3 — Authorized Notarial Acts and Fees		
State	**Authorized Acts Include****	**Maximum Fees**
AK	Acknowledgments; oaths and affirmations; jurats; attest documents; protests.	Fees not set by law but by individual Notary. Limited Governmental Notaries may not charge.
AL	Acknowledgments and proofs; oaths and affirmations; protests; "exercise such other powers as, according to commercial usage or the laws of this state, may belong to notaries public."	$5 per notarial act.
Am. Samoa	Acknowledgments; oaths and affirmations; jurats; witness signatures; certify copies.	Ack. or jurat $10 per sig.; oath/aff. without sig. $20 per person; witness sig. $10; certify copy $5 per page, minimum $10 total.
AR	Acknowledgments and proofs; oaths and affirmations; affidavits and depositions; certify copies; make declarations and protests.	$5 per certificate and seal; each protest and record of same $5; notice of protest $5.
AZ*	Acknowledgments; oaths and affirmations; jurats; certify copies.	Ack. or jurat $2 per sig.; oath/aff. without sig. $2 per person; certify copy $2 per page; mileage, per diem allowed.
CA*	Acknowledgments and proofs; oaths and affirmations; jurats; depositions; protests (only by Notaries in financial institutions); certify copies of powers of attorney.	$10 per notarized sig.; oath/aff. $10 per person; $20 per deposition plus $5 for oath and $5 for certificate; certify copy power of atty. $10. Travel fee allowed.
CO*	Acknowledgments and proofs; oaths and affirmations; jurats on depositions, affidavits; certify copies; "perform any other act permitted by law" including protests.	$5 per paper document attested; $10 per electronic notarization.

Table 3 — Authorized Notarial Acts and Fees		
State	**Authorized Acts Include****	**Maximum Fees**
CT	Acknowledgments; oaths and affirmations; jurats; take depositions in civil or probate cases and issue subpoenas for appearance of witnesses.	$5 per notarial act plus 35 cents per mile traveled.
DC	Acknowledgments and proofs; oaths and affirmations; verifications upon oath or affirmation; witness/attest signatures; protests.	$2 per notarial act.
DE	Acknowledgments; oaths and affirmations; verifications upon oath or affirmation; witness/attest signatures; certify/attest copies; protests.	$5 per "paper notarial act"; $25 per "electronic notarial act."
FL*	Acknowledgments; oaths and affirmations; jurats; certify copies; witness opening of safe deposit boxes; solemnize marriages; verify vehicle VIN numbers.	$10 per notarial act; $20 to verify VIN number; $30 per marriage.
GA*	Acknowledgments; oaths and affirmations; witness/attest signatures; verifications upon oath or affirmation; certify copies; other acts authorized by statute.	$2 per notarial act.
Guam	Acknowledgments; oaths and affirmations; jurats; copy certifications.	$10 for each of first two sigs. notarized, $8 for each additional; $10 per copy certified. "Reasonable" travel fees allowed. Guam gov. employee can't charge.

Table 3 — Authorized Notarial Acts and Fees		
State	**Authorized Acts Include****	**Maximum Fees**
HI*	Acknowledgments; oaths and affirmations; jurats; witness signatures; protests; certify copies of notarial records.	Ack. $5 per signer for original and duplicate, plus $2.50 for each subsequent dup.; jurat $5 for original and four dups. plus $2.50 for each subsequent. $5 for any other certificate. No fee for loyalty oath. Hawaii gov. employee can't charge.
IA	Acknowledgments and proofs; oaths and affirmations; verifications upon oath or affirmation; witness/attest signatures; certify/attest copies; protests.	"Reasonable fee" for notarial services.
ID	Acknowledgments and proofs; oaths and affirmations; certify copies; certify affidavits or depositions by jurat or verification; other acts permitted by law.	$2 per notarial act. Travel fee allowed.
IL*	Acknowledgments and proofs; oaths and affirmations; verifications upon oath or affirmation; witness/attest signatures	$1 per notarial act. (***Until July 1, 2018, up to $25 for acts related to certain Cook County conveyances — see footnote.)
IN	Acknowledgments and proofs; oaths and affirmations; affidavits or depositions by jurat; protests.	$2 per notarial act.
KS	Acknowledgments; oaths and affirmations; verifications upon oath or affirmation; witness/attest signatures; certify/attest copies; protests; other acts allowed by law.	"Reasonable fee" for any notarial act.
KY	Acknowledgments and proofs; oaths and affirmations; "attest documents"; depositions; protests.	Ack. $.50; recording act in book $.75; oath and certificate $.20; protest $.50, each notice $.25.

Table 3 — Authorized Notarial Acts and Fees		
State	**Authorized Acts Include****	**Maximum Fees**
LA	Acknowledgments; oaths and affirmations; certify copies; inventories, appraisements, and partitions; "receive wills, make protests, matrimonial contracts, conveyances, and generally, all contracts and instruments of writing"; hold family meetings and meetings of creditors; affidavits of correction; affix seals upon effects of deceased.	No statutory fee schedule.
MA*	Acknowledgments; oaths and affirmations; jurats; witness signatures; certify copies; issue summonses and subpoenas as provided by law.	No statutory fee schedule. "Reasonable cost" urged by officials.
MD	Acknowledgments; oaths and affirmations; "protests and declarations"; depositions; certify copies of notarial records; witness signings.	$4 for any "original notarial act." Travel fee allowed.
ME	Acknowledgments and proofs; oaths and affirmations; jurats; certify copies; protests; witness election petitions, absentee ballots; solemnize marriages; issue subpoenas and call meetings; witness opening of safe deposit boxes.	No statutory fee schedule, except $1.50 for protest.
MI*	Acknowledgments; oaths and affirmations; verifications upon oath or affirmation; witness/attest signatures.	$10 per notarial act. Travel fee allowed.
MN*	Acknowledgments; oaths and affirmations; verifications upon oath or affirmation; depositions; witness/attest signatures; certify/attest copies; protests.	$1 per notarial act.

Table 3 — Authorized Notarial Acts and Fees		
State	**Authorized Acts Include****	**Maximum Fees**
MO*	Acknowledgments and proofs; oaths and affirmations; jurats; certify copies; perform any other act permitted by law.	$2 per ack. or jurat sig. or copy certified but $1 for journal page copy by court order; $1 for oath/aff. apart from jurat; any other act $1. Travel fee allowed.
MS*	Acknowledgments; oaths and affirmations; jurats; signature witnessings; protests.	$5 maximum or $2 minimum per notarial act. Travel fee allowed.
MT*	Acknowledgments; oaths and affirmations; verifications upon oath or affirmation; witness/attest signatures; certify/attest copies; take depositions, affidavits; protests.	$5 per notarial act but $1 per ack. sig. after 1st; taking deposition, affidavit, other paper $3.50 per page. Travel fee allowed.
NC*	Acknowledgments; oaths and affirmations; "verifications or proofs".	$5 per notarial act. Electronic notaries may charge $10 per notarial act.
ND	Acknowledgments and proofs; oaths and affirmations; verifications upon oath or affirmation; witness/attest signatures; certify/attest copies; protests.	$5 per notarial act. Travel fee allowed.
NE*	Acknowledgments and proofs; oaths and affirmations; jurats; protests; depositions.	Ack. $5; oath/aff. $2; jurat $2; protest $1 but recording $2 and each notice $2. State employee can't charge. Travel fee allowed.
NH*	Acknowledgments; oaths and affirmations; verifications upon oath or affirmation; witness/attest signatures; certify/attest copies; protests; depositions; witness opening of safe deposit boxes.	$10 per notarial act.
NJ*	Acknowledgments and proofs; oaths and affirmations; jurats; protests; witness opening of safe deposit boxes.	$2.50 per notarial act. Certain acts related to real estate transfer or finance $15 or $25.

Table 3 — Authorized Notarial Acts and Fees		
State	**Authorized Acts Include****	**Maximum Fees**
NM*	Acknowledgments; oaths and affirmations; jurats; certify copies; witness/attest signatures; protests; any other act authorized by law.	$5 per notarial act; certify copy 50 cents per page but $5 min. Electronic act $10. Travel fee allowed.
N. Mariana Islands	Acknowledgments and proofs; oaths and affirmations; jurats; certify copies; protests; take depositions and affidavits.	Ack. $2 per person plus $2 for each duplicate original; oath/aff. with any jurat $2 plus $1 per dup. orig.; certify copy $2; mercantile protest $2, with notice $2; other protest $4, with notice $4; deposition $2 each.
NV*	Acknowledgments and proofs; oaths and affirmations; jurats; certify copies; protests; solemize marriages; other acts prescribed by law.	Ack. $5 plus $2.50 for each sig. after 1st; jurat $5 per sig.; oath/aff $2.50; certify copy $2.50; $75 per marriage. Travel fee allowed.
NY*	Acknowledgments and proofs; oaths and affirmations; jurats; protests; take depositions; witness opening of safe deposit boxes.	Ack. or proof $2 per person, plus $2 for each sworn witness; oath/aff. including any jurat $2 per person; protest 75 cents plus 10 cents per notice, not exceeding 5 notices.
OH*	Acknowledgments; oaths and affirmations; jurats for affidavits; protests.	Ack. $2; oath/aff. $2; jurat on affidavit including oath $1.50; protest $1 plus expenses.
OK	Acknowledgments and proofs; oaths and affirmations; verifications upon oath or affirmation; witness/attest signatures; certify/attest copies; protests.	$5 per notarial act.
OR*	Acknowledgments; oaths and affirmations; verifications upon oath or affirmation; witness/attest signatures; certify/attest copies; protests.	$10 per notarial act. Travel fee allowed.

Table 3 — Authorized Notarial Acts and Fees		
State	**Authorized Acts Include****	**Maximum Fees**
PA*	Acknowledgments; oaths and affirmations; jurats; certify copies; take depositions; protests; perform functions for vehicle title transfers if qualified by Penn. Dept. of Transportation.	Ack $5 plus $2 for each sig. after 1st; oath/aff. $5 per person; jurat on affidavit $5 for any no. of signers; certify copy $5; protest or deposition $3 per page.
P. Rico	In addition to powers of U.S. Notaries (acknowledgments, oaths, etc.) Puerto Rico Notaries have considerable attorney-like powers of Civil Law Notaries, as suggested above by description of the duties of Louisiana Notaries.	**** See footnote.
RI*	Acknowledgments; oaths and affirmations; jurats; witness signatures; certify copies; protests.	$1 per notarial act; jurat for affidavit 25 cents; for travel per mile, 10 cents. ***** See footnote for protests.
SC	Acknowledgments and proofs; oaths and affirmations; take depositions; protests; solemnize marriages; take renunciation of dower; witness opening of safe deposit boxes.	Every notarial certificate, with seal 50 cents; oath for affidavit 25 cents; taking deposition, swearing witnesses 25 cents per page; duplicating deposition, protest 10 cents per 100 words; protest, 50 cents plus postage costs and 50 cents per attendance; taking renunciation of dower $1.
SD	Acknowledgments and proofs; oaths and affirmations; jurats on affidavits and other sworn documents.	$10 per notarial act.. No fee for notarizing absentee ballot request.
TN*	Acknowledgments and proofs; oaths and affirmations; take depositions; jurats on affidavits; "qualify parties to bills in chancery."	$5 for ack., certifying copy or affixing seal — same as county clerk fees.

Table 3 — Authorized Notarial Acts and Fees		
State	**Authorized Acts Include****	**Maximum Fees**
TX*	Acknowledgments and proofs; oaths and affirmations; take depositions; certify copies; protests.	Ack. or proof $6 for 1st sig. plus $1 for each additional; oath/aff. with or without certificate $6; certify copy $6; take deposition $6 for oath, certificate, plus 50 cents per 100 words; protest $4, certificate $4, each notice $1.
UT*	Acknowledgments and proofs; oaths and affirmations; jurats; certify copies.	$5 per signature for ack., proof or jurat; oath/aff. without signature $5; certify copy $5 per page. Travel fee allowed.
VA*	Acknowledgments and proofs; oaths and affirmations; certify copies; jurats on affidavits and depositions; verifications of fact; witness opening of safe deposit boxes.	$5 per notarial act. $25 per electronic act. Travel fee allowed.
Virgin Islands, U.S.	Acknowledgments; oaths and affirmations; protests; perform other acts authorized by law.	$5 per notarial act. Separate fees for protests.
VT	Acknowledgments; oaths and affirmations; certify copies; protests; take affidavits, depositions; issue subpoenas for witnesses, deponents; witness opening of safe deposit boxes.	Each certificate under seal 50 cents; each protest under seal and notices $2.
WA*	Acknowledgments; oaths and affirmation; verifications upon oath or affirmation; witness/attest signatures; certify/attest copies; certify event or act; protests.	$10 per notarial act. Travel fee allowed.
WI	Acknowledgments; oaths and affirmations; verifications upon oath or affirmation; witness/attest signatures; certify/attest copies; protests.	Ack. and other services authorized by law 50 cents; protests required by law $1; other protests 50 cents.

Table 3 — Authorized Notarial Acts and Fees		
State	**Authorized Acts Include****	**Maximum Fees**
WV	Acknowledgments and proofs; oaths and affirmations; certify copies; perform other acts permitted by law.	$2 per notarial act. State employees may not charge.
WY	Acknowledgments; oaths and affirmations; jurats; witness/attest signatures; certify/attest copies; protests; perform other acts authorized by law.	Through June 30, 2014: $2 per notarial act. Effective July 1, 2014: $5 per notarial act. Travel fee allowed.

* A complete *Notary Law Primer* is published for this state by the National Notary Association. Each such *Primer* is devoted exclusively to an in-depth examination of the statutes, regulations, rulings, directives and customs governing Notaries in the one state.

** For each state, these are the most common and regularly performed notarial acts for the majority of Notaries, but not necessarily all of the acts that may be authorized by law in a given state. For example, some states empower Notaries to execute proofs based on recognition of handwriting, but this act is rarely performed.

*** A statutory program imposes special duties on Illinois Notaries who notarize "Documents of Conveyance" for "Residential Real Property" in Cook County (5 ILCS 312/3-102). Established in 2008 by Public Act 988, this antifraud program is in effect from June 1, 2009, through July 1, 2018.

**** Fees for Puerto Rico Notaries Public are: "For notarizing public instruments concerning valuables not exceeding $10,000 in value: $150; For notarizing public instruments concerning valuables between $10,000 and $5,000,000 in value: fee fixed by agreement between the parties and the Notary but never more than 1% or less than 0.5% of the value, and never less than $250; For notarizing public instruments concerning valuables exceeding $5,000,000 in value: same fee as above plus the fee fixed by agreement between the parties and the Notary on the amount exceeding $5,000,000; For notarizing public instruments concerning nonvaluables: fee fixed by agreement between the parties and the Notary but never less than $150; For notarizing testimonies and sworn statements and for authenticating signatures or affidavits: fee fixed by agreement between the parties and the Notary; For issuing certified copies of deeds: fee based on document's amount, excluding costs, expenses and disbursements, as follows: from $0 to $10,000 — $15; from $10,001 to $500,000 — $25; over $500,000 — $40.

***** For protests, the maximum fees for Rhode Island Notaries Public are: extending and recording a marine protest $1.50; recording a protest for nonacceptance or nonpayment, if amount involved is $500 dollars or more, $1; if less than $500, 50 cents; noting nonacceptance or nonpayment, 25 cents; for each notice given to a party liable for payment, 25 cents. "(T)he whole cost of protest, including necessary notices and the record, shall not exceed two dollars ($2.00), and the whole cost of noting, including notices, shall in no case exceed one dollar and twenty-five cents."

PRACTICES AND PROCEDURES

Identifying Document Signers

Procedure. The identity of a document signer is established either through the Notary's own personal knowledge of the signer, or through what is widely known as satisfactory evidence.

Satisfactory evidence is defined either as proof by identification documents or by the vouching under oath or affirmation of one or two credible identifying witnesses.

Personal Knowledge of Identity

Definition. Personal knowledge is having an acquaintance derived from association with the individual in relation to other people over a period of time. The longer the Notary has known someone, the safer it is to rely on personal knowledge as a method of identification.

A good friend from school known for several years might be considered personally known, while an informal introduction of a stranger by a coworker or employer does not constitute personal knowledge. The general rule to follow is that if there is any doubt about whether the individual is personally known, consider the person unknown for purposes of notarization and request another form of identification.

Identification through personal knowledge is acceptable in many states. In California, however, personal knowledge may not be used as a sole means of identification.

Identification Documents

Acceptable Identification Documents. Identification documents should be government-issued and contain the bearer's recent photograph, as well as the individual's signature and physical description. Common identification documents include state drivers' licenses and non-driver IDs, and federal passports.

Some states have laws or rules that either list acceptable identification documents or outline required features. Be sure to know the requirements for your state, which may be found in the table that follows this section on identification or through your state's Notary regulating office.

Unacceptable Identification Documents. Best practice dictates that Social Security cards, credit cards, temporary driver licenses and driver licenses without photographs not be relied on for identification purposes. Some states expressly prohibit their use by Notaries.

Fraudulent Identification Documents. A Notary should inspect the identification document to see if it might have been altered. The Notary is not expected to be a master at detecting fraudulent documents, however, a simple examination often reveals alterations.

As a Notary, you should become familiar with the most common types of identification documents you will encounter in your state. This familiarity makes it easier to spot discrepancies and detect fraudulent identification. Ask the signer to remove the card from his or her wallet or any protective casing so that you may hold the card as you examine it.

Here are some clues to spotting a possibly fraudulent ID:

- The signer lacks familiarity with the information on the ID.
- There are misspelled words in the standard printed language.
- There are unlikely similarities between cards (e.g., same photograph).
- The card bears typed or handwritten insertions.
- There are raised edges around a photograph.
- Official seals or signatures are covered.
- There are smudges, erasures or inconsistencies in color or texture.
- The signature on the ID card looks different from that on the document or in the Notary's journal.

If you suspect the identification document is fraudulent, refuse to perform the notarization.

Credible Identifying Witnesses

Definition. A Notary may rely on the word of a credible identifying witness to identify an unknown document signer if this witness is personally known to the Notary and has taken an oath or affirmation from the Notary to compel truthfulness. In most states, the sworn word of a credible witness is regarded as satisfactory evidence of identity and legally equivalent to personal knowledge. In a sense, a credible witness is a walking, talking ID card.

A credible identifying witness must personally know the document signer and be personally known by the Notary or, in some states, identified by the Notary through acceptable identification documents. In California, such a witness must present acceptable ID cards, since personal knowledge alone will not suffice.

For example, if a stranger without satisfactory IDs requests a notarization, the Notary need not turn this person away if the Notary has a friend present who personally knows the individual. The friend could serve as a credible identifying witness.

By definition, a credible identifying witness is a believable person. Credible identifying witnesses should be honest, competent and impartial to the matter at hand. This means that the credible identifying witness should neither have a beneficial interest in a notarized document nor be named in it.

Oath for a Credible Identifying Witness. To compel truthfulness, the Notary must administer an oath or affirmation to the credible identifying witness. The identifying witness must swear or affirm that the signer has the identity claimed.

If not otherwise prescribed by law, the following oath (or affirmation) may be used:

> Do you solemnly swear (or affirm) that you know the signer truly holds the identity he (or she) claims?

The oath or affirmation must be spoken aloud, and the credible identifying witness must answer affirmatively with, "I do," "Yes," or a similar response that indicates agreement.

Two Credible Witnesses. To identify a document signer, some states have the option of relying on two credible identifying witnesses who are not personally known by the Notary, as long as both have acceptable IDs.

Know the exact rules for credible identifying witnesses in your state.

Willingness and Awareness

Purpose. The Notary screens for willingness to verify that the signing appears to be a voluntary act, freely made, without duress or undue influence.

Procedure. When screening for awareness, the Notary checks that the signer appears to understand the document. Notaries are expected only to make a layperson's commonsense judgment about a signer's awareness.

If the Notary suspects that a signer is being coerced or pressured into signing or is unable to respond coherently to the Notary's basic questions, the Notary should refuse to perform the notarization. Sometimes it may be necessary to ask a third party to leave the room during the questioning, particularly if it appears that third party is coaching or influencing the signer.

Representative Capacity

Verification. Some states require signers to present documentation proving that they are authorized to sign in a representative capacity such as partner, trustee, president of a corporation or attorney in fact. It is a good practice to confirm with the signer that he or she has the authorization to sign in this capacity and note that confirmation in the additional comments field of the journal of notarial acts.

In some states, such as California, Notaries need only identify an acknowledging signer as an individual and not as a representative.

Table 4 — Methods of Identification

State	Personal Knowledge	One Personally Known Credible Identifying Witness	Two Credible Identifying Witnesses with ID Documents	Acceptable Identification Documents
AK	Permitted	Not specified	Not specified	Gov. issued w/ photo and sig.; or gov. issued w/sig. plus another valid ID w/photo and sig.
AL	Not specified	Not specified	Not specified	Not specified
Am. Samoa	Permitted	Permitted	Permitted	Gov. issued w/ photo, sig. and phys. description. Duly stamped passport okay. ID issued by recognized Indian tribe.

Table 4 — Methods of Identification

State	Personal Knowledge	One Personally Known Credible Identifying Witness	Two Credible Identifying Witnesses with ID Documents	Acceptable Identification Documents
AR	Permitted	Not specified	Not specified	"Require some form of proper identification unless the notary personally recognizes the person whose signature is to be notarized." — Ark. Notary Public Handbook
AZ*	Permitted	Permitted; ID card identification of witnesses also allowed	Not specified	Unexpired driver license, US passport or military ID or other ID issued by US, state or tribal gov. w/photo, sig. and phys. description. Other IDs allowed for real estate docs.
CA*	Not Permitted	Only if known witness also presents acceptable ID document	Permitted	Current or issued in last 5 years, w/ photo, phys. description, sig. and ID number. DL issued by any state or by Can. or Mex., ID card issued by any state, US or foreign passport, US military ID, employee ID issued by agency or office of CA, inmate ID card issued by CDCR.

Table 4 — Methods of Identification				
State	**Personal Knowledge**	**One Personally Known Credible Identifying Witness**	**Two Credible Identifying Witnesses with ID Documents**	**Acceptable Identification Documents**
CO*	Permitted	Permitted	Not specified	Current ID issued by federal or state gov. w/photo and sig. Foreign passport not acceptable.
CT	Permitted	Permitted	Not specified	Two current IDs: 1st is fed. or state issued w/sig. and photo or phys. description; 2nd is from institution, business or fed./ state gov. w/sig.
DC	Permitted	Permitted	Not specified	Permitted but without statutory specifications.
DE	Permitted	Permitted	Permitted	Gov. issued ID w/ photo and sig. including US and foreign passports, driver licenses, mil. IDs.
FL*	Permitted	Permitted	Permitted	Specified gov. IDs current or issued in last 5 years w/ID number, including state, Mex. or Can. driver licenses; US or foreign passports; military, immigrant or inmate IDs.
GA*	Permitted	Permitted	Permitted	Any state, Mex. or Can. driver license or non-driver ID; US or foreign passport; military ID; resident alien card.

Table 4 — Methods of Identification				
State	**Personal Knowledge**	**One Personally Known Credible Identifying Witness**	**Two Credible Identifying Witnesses with ID Documents**	**Acceptable Identification Documents**
Guam	Permitted	Not specified	Not specified	Current US or foreign passport; any ID issued by US or state gov. w/ photo and sig.
HI*	Permitted	Permitted	Not specified	Current ID of US, state or foreign federal gov. w/ photo and sig.
IA	Permitted	Permitted	Not specified	Best IDs are gov. issued w/photo, sig., phys. description, including driver license, passport, school or work card.
ID	Permitted	Permitted	Not specified	Reliable current photo ID such as driver license, passport or military card.
IL*	Permitted	Permitted	Not specified	Current state or federal government ID w/photo and sig.
IN	Permitted	Permitted	Not specified	ID such as driver license okay — no further specifications.
KS	Permitted	Permitted	Not specified	Reliable ID includes photo such as driver license.
KY	Permitted	Not specified	Not specified	ID should have photo, sig., phys. description.
LA	Not specified	Not specified	Not specified	Not specified. Notary has broad discretion in determining proof of identity.

Table 4 — Methods of Identification

State	Personal Knowledge	One Personally Known Credible Identifying Witness	Two Credible Identifying Witnesses with ID Documents	Acceptable Identification Documents
MA*	Permitted	Permitted	Not specified	Current, issued by federal or state agency w/photo and sig. For non-citizen, foreign passport or other gov. ID.
MD	Permitted	Not specified	Not specified	"(R)equire such proof of identification as (Notary) would require to cash a very large check for that person."
ME	Permitted	Permitted	Not specified	Current gov. issued IDs w/photo and phys. description recommended.
MI*	Permitted	Permitted	Not specified	Current, issued by federal or state agency w/photo and sig.
MN*	Permitted	Permitted	Not specified	ID documents permitted but law provides no specifications.
MO*	Permitted	Permitted	2 witnesses for real estate but ID method not specified	Best ID has photo and sig. such as driver license.
MS*	Permitted	Permitted	Permitted	Current, issued by federal, state or tribal agency w/ photo, sig., phys. description. Properly stamped passport also acceptable.
MT*	Permitted	Permitted	Not specified	Current ID w/photo and sig.

Table 4 — Methods of Identification				
State	**Personal Knowledge**	**One Personally Known Credible Identifying Witness**	**Two Credible Identifying Witnesses with ID Documents**	**Acceptable Identification Documents**
NC*	Permitted	Permitted	Not specified	Current federal, state or tribal gov. ID w/ photo and either sig. or phys. description.
ND	Permitted	Permitted; ID card identification also allowed	Not specified	ID current or expired no more than 3 yrs.; passport, driver or nondriver ID, or other gov.-issued ID w/ photo or sig.
NE*	Permitted	Permitted	Permitted	Current, gov.-issued ID card w/photo, sig. and phys. description. Properly stamped passport acceptable.
NH*	Permitted	Permitted	Not specified	Consult list of acceptable IDs in elections laws, which includes federal, state and local IDs w/photos. Allows employer photo IDs if known to be reliable.
NJ*	Permitted	Permitted	Not specified	At least one form of ID that contains physical description.
NM*	Permitted	Permitted	Permitted	Current federal, state or tribal ID w/photo, sig. and phys. description. Duly stamped passport okay.

Table 4 — Methods of Identification

State	Personal Knowledge	One Personally Known Credible Identifying Witness	Two Credible Identifying Witnesses with ID Documents	Acceptable Identification Documents
N. Mar. Islands	Permitted	Permitted	Not specified	At least 2 current IDs: 1st issued by government w/ photo, sig. and phys. description; 2nd by institution, business or federal or state gov. w/sig.
NV*	Permitted	Permitted	Not specified	ID w/photo and sig. Consul-issued card okay.
NY*	Permitted	Not specified	Not specified	Not specified
OH*	Permitted	Permitted	Not specified	Driver license or other ID, "preferably one with a picture."
OK	Permitted	Permitted	Not specified	"Proper ID should include a photograph and signature such as a driver's license or passport." -- FAQ, state website
OR*	Permitted	Permitted	Not specified	Current or expired no more than 3 years: ID card or DL issued by any state, OR instructional driver's permit, OR provisional DL, OR limited-term DL or ID card, US or foreign passport; current or expired no more than 3 years with photo and sig.: US military ID, government-issued ID, ID issued by recognized Indian tribe; current (not expired): OR interim DL or ID card.

Table 4 — Methods of Identification				
State	**Personal Knowledge**	**One Personally Known Credible Identifying Witness**	**Two Credible Identifying Witnesses with ID Documents**	**Acceptable Identification Documents**
PA*	Permitted	Permitted	Not specified	Current, gov.-issued ID w/photo or sig. or phys. description and ID number.
P. Rico	Permitted	Permitted	Not specified	ID w/photo and sig. issued by competent public authority of Puerto Rico, US federal gov. or state; foreign passport.
RI*	Permitted	Permitted	Not specified	Current ID issued by federal, state or tribal gov. w/photo and sig. For non-US citizens — valid passport or other gov.-issued ID w/ photo and sig.
SC	Permitted	Permitted	Not specified	Valid driver license or state ID; US military ID; or passport.
SD	Permitted	Permitted	Not specified	Driver license or non-driver ID; US passport; military ID; or ID issued by USCIS, such as Resident Alien card.
TN*	Permitted	Permitted	Not specified	Current or issued in last 5 years w/photo, phys. description, sig. and ID number; US or foreign passport; state driver license or ID; military ID.

Table 4 — Methods of Identification				
State	**Personal Knowledge**	**One Personally Known Credible Identifying Witness**	**Two Credible Identifying Witnesses with ID Documents**	**Acceptable Identification Documents**
TX*	Permitted	Permitted	Not specified	Current ID issued by federal or state gov. w/photo and sig. For residential real estate transaction, current foreign passport suffices.
UT*	Permitted	Permitted	Not specified	ID issued by US, state or foreign gov. w/photo, phys. description and sig. Valid passport issued by any nation okay.
VA*	Permitted	Permitted	Permitted	ID w/photo and sig.: US or foreign passport; state driver license or ID; US military card; US cert. of citizenship or naturalization; alien registration card.
Virgin Islands, U.S.	Permitted	Not specified	Not specified	"The best form of identification is one which includes a photograph and signature. A valid driver's license is a good source of identification." – Notary Public Handbook

Table 4 — Methods of Identification

State	Personal Knowledge	One Personally Known Credible Identifying Witness	Two Credible Identifying Witnesses with ID Documents	Acceptable Identification Documents
VT	Permitted	Permitted	Not specified	"If you don't know the person to be who he or she claims to be, you... may refuse to act (or) (y)ou may rely on a credible witness who is personally known to you." — Vermont Notary Guide
WA*	Permitted	Permitted	Not specified	Current federal or state gov. ID w/ photo, sig. and phys. description.
WI	Permitted	Permitted	Not specified	"A current driver's license, photo identification card, picture credit card, student ID card, or employment ID may be enough proof for you to establish … identity." — Tutorial
WV	Permitted	Not specified	Not specified	"(A)sk for a driver's license or some other form of identification." — West Virginia Notary Handbook
WY	Permitted	Permitted	Permitted	Federal, state or tribal agency issued ID w/photo, sig. and physical description. Properly stamped passport is acceptable.

* A complete *Notary Law Primer* is published for this state by the National Notary Association. Each such *Primer* is devoted exclusively to an in-depth examination of the statutes, regulations, rulings, directives and customs governing Notaries in the one state.

Journal of Notarial Acts

Requirement. Many states by law require Notaries Public to keep some form of record, whether it be for all acts or for certain acts such as protests. Yet, virtually all states recommend that Notaries keep a journal of all notarial acts, recognizing that as a prudent, commonsense thing to do and a sound business practice.

Format. To be most effective, the journal should have bound pages, not loose-leaf, and the pages should be numbered to deter unauthorized removal. In addition, it is important that notarial acts be recorded chronologically, since this can point out later tampering with the dates of notarization.

Entries. States that require a Notary to keep and maintain a journal may or may not have laws specifying what information must be recorded. At the very least, the NNA recommends as a best practice that the following be recorded. You should check your own state's specific requirements.

- Date and time of notarial act
- Type of notarial act
- Title or type of document
- Document date
- Name and address of each signer and witness
- Method of identification
- Fees charged
- Signature of each signer and witness
- Thumbprint for every notarization (not permitted in some states)

- Other pertinent information, such as the printed names of signers, the representative capacity (if any) of the signer, and the address where the notarization was performed.

Copying by Employer. In the absence of specific rules in law, it is generally considered a fair policy for an employer of a Notary to inspect or copy Notary journal entries that are directly related to the employer's business, if the inspection or copying is done in the Notary's presence. An employer may ask a Notary-employee to regularly provide copies of business-related entries from the journal. The Notary shall not be required to allow inspection or provide copies of journal entries that are not related to the employer's business. A few states (e.g., Arizona) have statutes allowing law firms that employ Notaries to exert greater control over Notary journals because of the considerations of attorney-client privilege.

Surrendering Journal. Notaries should never surrender control of their official journals to anyone. Even when an employer has paid for the Notary's official journal — regardless of whether the journal contains entries related to the employer's business — the journal stays with the Notary upon termination of employment. The Notary must not surrender a journal to anyone unless subpoenaed by court order.

Lost or Stolen Journal. Depending upon state laws, it is a good policy for the Notary to immediately notify the Notary commissioning authority by certified or registered mail if a journal is lost, stolen, misplaced, destroyed, damaged or otherwise rendered unusable.

Disposal of Notary Records. When a Notary commission is resigned, revoked, or expires without renewal, a Notary may be required to turn in all Notary records to a designated official.

If your state laws do not require that you submit the journal to a designated official upon commission termination, it is recommended that you safeguard each journal for ten years from the date of the last recorded entry.

Notary Certificate

Requirement. In notarizing any document, a Notary must complete a notarial certificate. Many states have laws that stipulate specific certificate wording for each type of notarial act. Other states prescribe no wording at all and allow for a range of certificates. Notarial certificates come in one of two physical formats:

- Preprinted Certificates: The wording is preprinted on the document itself.

- 'Loose' Certificates: The Notary attaches a so-called "loose" certificate to a document in instances when certificate wording is not printed on the document, does not comply with state requirements or when multiple signers have their signatures notarized at different times.

Certificate Contents. The certificate is wording that indicates exactly what the Notary has certified. The certificate should contain:

1) A venue indicating where the notarization is performed. "State of ______, County of _______," is the typical venue wording, with the state and county name inserted in the blanks. The letters "SS." or "SCT." sometimes appear after the venue; they abbreviate the traditional Latin word *scilicet*, meaning "in particular" or "namely."

2) A statement of particulars indicating exactly what the notarization has attested. An acknowledgment certificate would include such wording as:

   "On __________ before me, (here insert name and title of the officer), personally appeared _____________, who proved to me on the basis of satisfactory evidence to be the person(s)..."

   A jurat certificate would include such wording as:

   "Subscribed and sworn to (or affirmed) before me on this ______ day of ___________ (month), _____ (year), by _______________, proved to me on the basis of satisfactory evidence to be the person(s) ... "

   The statement of particulars often includes wording that the Notary must line through or cross out — for example "he/she/they" when referring to the signer(s). The Notary must line through the inapplicable extra words or circle the applicable words.

3) A testimonium clause, which may be optional if the date is

included in the statement of particulars: "Witness my hand and official seal, this _______ day of __________ (month), ____ (year)." In this short sentence, the Notary formally attests to the truthfulness of the preceding facts in the certificate. "Hand" means signature.

4) The official signature of the Notary, exactly as the name appears on the Notary's commission.

5) The official seal of the Notary. On many certificates the letters "L.S." appear, indicating where the seal is to be located. These letters abbreviate the Latin term *locus sigilli*, meaning "place of the seal." An inking seal should be placed near but not over the letters, so that wording imprinted by the seal will not be obscured. An embossing seal, used in conjunction with an inking seal, may be placed directly over the letters — slightly displacing portions of the characters and leaving a clue that document examiners can use to distinguish an original from a forged photocopy.

In addition to the Notary's official signature and seal, some states may also require additional information to be added such as the Notary's commission number, commission expiration date or the county where the Notary's commission is recorded if this information does not appear on the seal.

Loose Certificates. When certificate wording is not preprinted on the document, a loose certificate may be attached by the Notary. This form is typically stapled to the signature page's left margin. To prevent a loose certificate from being removed and fraudulently placed on another document, there are precautions a Notary can take. The Notary can emboss the certificate and document together, writing "attached document bears embossment" on the certificate, or write a brief description of the document on the certificate: "This certificate is attached to a __________ (title or type of document), dated __________, of __________ (number) pages, signed by __________ (name[s] of signer[s])."

While fraud-deterrent steps such as these can make it much more difficult for a loose certificate to be removed and misused, there is no absolute protection against its removal and misuse. Notaries must ensure that, while a certificate remains in their control, it is attached only to the intended document.

Correcting a Notary Certificate. If the preprinted venue or other wording is inaccurate, you may correct the wording by lining through it, writing the correct location or other information, then initialing and dating the change.

Do Not Pre-Sign/Seal Certificates. A Notary must never sign and/or seal certificates ahead of time or permit other persons to attach loose notarial certificates to documents. Also, the Notary should not send an unattached, signed and sealed loose certificate through the mail, even if requested to do so by a signer who previously appeared before the Notary. These actions may facilitate fraud or forgery, and they could subject the Notary to lawsuits to recover damages resulting from the Notary's neglect or misconduct.

Notary Seal

Purpose. The seal signifies that the Notary is a public officer commissioned in a particular state. Depending on state law, your seal may also provide certain other information about you, such as the county where your Notary commission, bond and oath of office may be on file, as well as the commission number and expiration date.

Types of Seals. The two main types of official seal are the modern rubber or plastic inking stamp and the traditional metal embosser.

The most common seal is an inking stamp, which imprints a photographically reproducible image on the document. The embosser is a metal pincer-like device, which imprints an image in relief on a paper surface.

Disposing of the Seal. When a Notary's term of office ends, you must destroy or deface the official seal unless your state laws prescribe a different method of disposal, such as submitting the seal to your Notary-regulating office.

Securing the Journal and Seal. Always store your journal and seal under lock and key. Only you, the Notary, may lawfully use your journal and seal. If you change jobs, the journal and seal go with you, regardless of who paid for them. These tools are the exclusive property of the Notary. If the journal or seal is stolen, lost, destroyed or damaged, notify the state's Notary-regulating office — and local police, if appropriate.

Journal and Seal Requirements

In all states where Notaries are not required by law to maintain a journal of their official acts, virtually all Notary-regulating authorities nonetheless recommend the keeping of a journal.

For instance, the Alaska Lieutenant Governor's website ("Frequently Asked Questions") states:

"You are not required by law to keep permanent record of your notarizations, however, this office cannot emphasize enough the importance of recording every notarization you perform in a proper notary journal. Journal entries should be sequentially numbered and any journal or recording system where the pages are not physically bound together … in a manner that prevents them from being inserted or removed from the journal by the notary should be avoided."

For seals, the measurements indicated in the table below are maximums unless otherwise indicated. "Notary's name" indicates the name of the Notary Public exactly as it appears on his or her commission or appointment certificate.

In any state listed below where the Notary's commission expiration date does not appear in the seal, the Notary must always ensure that this critical date appears elsewhere on the notarial certificate in photocopiable form. Indeed, in states where seals are not required by law, officials direct Notaries to stamp, type or print the expiration date on the certificate, along with their name, state and title ("Notary Public"), creating thereby a "de facto seal" and acknowledging the seal's importance.

Table 5 — Journal and Seal Requirements

State	Journal	Seal	Seal Shape/Content
AK	Recommended	Inked stamp or photocopiable embosser	Circular, not over 2" in diameter; or rectangular, not over 1" high and 2 1/2" long w/Notary's name, "Notary Public" and "State of Alaska" (Optional: exp. date, comm. no.)
AL	Recommended	Inked stamp or embosser allowed	Notary's name, "Notary Public" and "Alabama" or "State of Alabama"

Table 5 — Journal and Seal Requirements			
State	**Journal**	**Seal**	**Seal Shape/Content**
Am. Samoa	Required	Inked stamp or adhesive label (embosser only allowed as add-on)	Rectangular, no larger than 1" x 2"; border surrounding Notary's name, com. no., "Notary Public", "Territory of American Samoa", "My commission expires (date)" and Notary's business address
AR	Recommended	Blue or black inked stamp or photocopiable embosser	Notary's name, county where bond filed, "Notary Public", "Arkansas", comm. exp. date, comm. no.
AZ*	Required	Dark-inked rubber stamp (not red). Embosser only allowed as add-on.	Any shape, but size no more than 1 ½" by 2 ½" w/Notary's name, "Notary Public", county, Arizona state seal, comm. exp. date
CA*	Required	Inked stamp or photocopiable embosser	Rectangular no larger than 1" by 2 ½", or circular 2" in diameter; serrated or milled edge border surrounding Notary's name, California state seal, "Notary Public", county where oath and bond filed, comm. exp. date, comm. no., seal manufacturer ID no.
CO*	Required	Inked rubber stamp or embosser	ONLY: Border around these words: Notary's name, "Notary Public", "State of Colorado", comm. no. and comm. exp. date.
CT	Recommended	Optional: embosser or inked stamp allowed	Notary's name, "Notary Public", "Connecticut", (Optional: "My commission expires (date)")

Table 5 — Journal and Seal Requirements			
State	**Journal**	**Seal**	**Seal Shape/Content**
DC	Required	Inked embosser	Circular w/diameter no larger than 1.75" around: at top Notary's name, in center "Notary Public" and comm. exp. date, at bottom "District of Columbia"
DE	Required only for electronic acts	Black-inked rubber stamp or photocopiable embosser	Notary's name, "Notary Public", "State of Delaware", "My commission expires on (date)" (For Limited Governmental Notaries: "My commission expires upon office")
FL*	Recommended	Black-inked rubber stamp (embosser only allowed as add-on)	Notary's name, "Notary Public – State of Florida", comm. no., comm. exp. date (Prohibited: Great Seal of Florida)
GA*	Recommended	Inked stamp or photocopiable embosser	Notary's name, "Notary Public", "Georgia" or "GA", county (Optional but urged by officials: comm. exp. date)
Guam	Required	2 seals mandatory: black-inked stamp and photocopiable embosser	Rectangular stamp — Notary's Name, "Notary Public in and for Guam, U.S.A.", "My commission expires (date)", Notary's business or residence address. Embosser — Notary's name, "Notary Public in and for Guam, U.S.A."
HI*	Required	Inked rubber stamp or photocopiable embosser	Circular, not over 2" in diameter; serrated or milled edge border; Notary's name, comm. no., "Notary Public", "State of Hawaii" **

Table 5 — Journal and Seal Requirements			
State	**Journal**	**Seal**	**Seal Shape/Content**
IA	Recommended	Inked stamp or photocopiable embosser	"Notarial Seal" and "Iowa", Notary's name, comm. no., "My commission expires (date)"
ID	Recommended	Inked rubber stamp	Rectangular or circular, serrated or milled edge border surrounding only the words: Notary's name, "Notary Public", "State of Idaho"
IL*	Not required but must keep fee record ***	Black-inked rubber stamp	No larger than 1" by 2 ½", serrated or milled edge border w/ "Official Seal", Notary's name, "Notary Public", "State of Illinois", "My commission expires (date)"
IN	Recommended	Inked stamp or photocopiable embosser	Notary's name (optional but preferred), "Notary Public", "State of Indiana" or "Indiana", "Seal" (Optional: comm. exp. date)
KS	Recommended	Inked rubber stamp or photocopiable embosser	Notary's name, "Notary Public", "State of Kansas", (Optional: comm. exp. date; picture of Kansas Capitol building)
KY	Recommended	Optional	If used any seal should contain Notary's name, either "Notary Public – State at Large" or "Notary Public – Special Commission" and "Kentucky"
LA	Annual report required	Optional	Notary must type, print or stamp name and identification no. (unless Notary is attorney, who would use state bar roll no.)

Table 5 — Journal and Seal Requirements			
State	**Journal**	**Seal**	**Seal Shape/Content**
MA*	Required	Black-inked stamp or embosser	Notary's name, "Notary Public", "Commonwealth of Massachusetts" or "Massachusetts", "My commission expires (date)", Great Seal of Mass.
MD	Required	Inked stamp or embosser	Notary's name, "Notary Public", Name of county or "City of Baltimore", "Maryland" or "MD" (Optional: "symbol or device" of Notary's choosing)
ME	Only requires record of marriages but it is recommended that Notaries keep records of all acts	Optional: inked stamp or embosser allowed	Notary's name, "Notary Public", Maine" or "ME" or Great Seal (not preferred)
MI*	Recommended	Optional: inked stamp or electronic process allowed (embosser only allowed as add-on)	If not in seal, this must be photocopiable: Notary's name, "Notary Public, State of Michigan, County of (name of county)", "My commission expires (date)." Also, if not redundant: "Acting in County of (county where notarization done)" and date
MN*	Recommended	Inked stamp	Rectangular, max. ¾" by 2 ½ inches; serrated or milled edge border w/ Notary's name, "Notary Public", Minnesota Great Seal, "My commission expires (date)"

Table 5 — Journal and Seal Requirements			
State	**Journal**	**Seal**	**Seal Shape/Content**
MO*	Required	Black-inked rubber stamp or embosser	Min. 8 pt. font. Inked stamp: Notary's name, "Notary Public", "Notary Seal", "State of Missouri", county where commissioned (or "St. Louis City"), "My commission expires (date)", comm. no. Embosser: Notary's name, "Notary Seal", "Notary Public", comm. no., "State of Missouri", plus certain info stamped, typed or printed photocopiably
MS*	Required	Inked stamp (embosser only allowed as add-on)	Circular, diameter at least 1 ½" or max. 2 ½"; a border surrounding Notary's name, "State of Mississippi", county of Notary's residence; across center, "Notary Public", comm. ID no. and "Commission expires (date)"
MT*	Required	Blue or black-inked seal-stamp unit	Rectangular, approx. 1" by 2 ½" containing circular seal w/Notary's name, "Notarial Seal" or "Notary Public", "State of Montana." Also required in rectangle: "Notary Public for the State of Montana", "Residing at (city where Notary lives)" and comm. exp. date expressed as month/day/four-digit year
NC*	Recommended	Inked stamp or photocopiable embosser	Circular between 1 ½" to 2" in diameter or rectangular max. 1" by 2 ½"; a border surrounding Notary's name, "Notary Public", county name w/ word "County" or "Co.", "North Carolina" or "NC" (Optional: comm. exp. date)

Table 5 — Journal and Seal Requirements			
State	**Journal**	**Seal**	**Seal Shape/Content**
ND	Recommended	Inked stamp device	Circular 1 5/8" in diameter or rectangular max. 7/8" by 2 5/8" w/Notary's name, "Notary Public", "State of North Dakota", comm. exp. date
NE*	Recommended	Inked stamp	Rectangular ½" by 2", or shaped like state, w/ Notary's name, "State of Nebraska", "General Notary" or "General Notarial", comm. exp. date
NH*	Recommended	Inked rubber stamp or embosser	Embosser: Notary's name, "Notary Public", "New Hampshire" and separate inked stamp with comm. exp. date. Inked stamp: Notary's name, "Notary Public", "New Hampshire", comm. exp. date
NJ*	Required by law for protest and for other acts by Div. of Revenue	Optional	Seal may be used to affix Notary's name and comm. exp. date, which are required by state.
NM*	Recommended	Inked rubber stamp or embosser	Embosser: Notary's name, "Notary Public—State of New Mexico". Inked Stamp: "Official Seal", Notary's name, "Notary Public – State of New Mexico", "My commission expires (date)", New Mexico Great Seal
N. Mar. Islands	Required	Inked rubber stamp or embosser	Rectangular or circular, max. 2" w/Notary's name, "Notary Public", "Commonwealth of the Northern Mariana Islands", Notary's business or residence address, "My commission expires (date)"

Table 5 — Journal and Seal Requirements			
State	**Journal**	**Seal**	**Seal Shape/Content**
NV*	Required	Inked rubber stamp or other mechanical or computer device (embosser only allowed as add-on)	Rectangular, max. 1" by 2 ½" w/Notary's name, "Notary Public, State of Nevada", appt. exp. date, appt. no., "Nonresident" if residing in adjoining state (Optional Nevada Great Seal)
NY*	Not required	Optional, but may be used to stamp certain required information. If stamp is used, must be black ink.	Notary must print, type or stamp following in black ink below signature: Notary's name, "Notary Public State of New York", county of Notary's original comm., comm. exp. date, if required county where Notary's cert. of official character filed
OH*	Required by law for protests	Inked stamp or embosser	Circular w/state coat of arms in center of 1" circle; a border surrounding "Notary Public" or "Notarial Seal", "State of Ohio" and Notary's name which may alternatively be printed, typed or stamped near signature
OK	Recommended	Inked rubber stamp or embosser	Notary's name, "Notary Public", "State of Oklahoma" (Optional: comm. no. and/or exp. date)
OR*	Required	Inked stamp (black or dark ink recommended). Embosser only allowed as add-on.	Oregon Great Seal in upper left corner of rectangle; w/words centered to right in descending order: "Official Seal", Notary's Name, "Notary Public — Oregon", "Commission No. (No.)", "My Commission Expires (date)" w/month spelled out, two digits for date and year four digits

Table 5 — Journal and Seal Requirements			
State	**Journal**	**Seal**	**Seal Shape/Content**
PA*	Required	Inked rubber stamp (embosser only allowed as add-on)	Rectangular, 1" by 3 ½" max. w/plain border surrounding: "Notarial Seal", Notary's name, "Notary Public", municipality and county of Notary's office, comm. exp. date (Optional: "Commonwealth of Pennsylvania" but must be outside top of border)
P. Rico	Not required; original documents kept	Inked stamp or embosser	Notary's name, "Abogado-Notario", "Puerto Rico" or "Isla de Puerto Rico", any icon of Notary's choice
RI*	Recommended	Optional: Inked stamp or photocopiable embosser	If seal used: Notary's name, "Notary Public", "Rhode Island" (Optional: comm. exp. date or other phrases such as "Signed before me")
SC	Recommended	Inked rubber stamp or embosser	Notary's name, "Notary Public" "South Carolina" (Optional: comm. exp. date)
SD	Recommended	Inked stamp or embosser	Border surrounding Notary's name, "Notary Public", "South Dakota", for inked stamps "Seal" (Optional: comm. exp. date)
TN*	Required	Inked stamp (not black or yellow but must appear black when photocopied)	Circular with 2 concentric circles: at top Notary's name, in middle "State of Tennessee Notary Public" or "Tennessee Notary Public", at bottom Notary's county
TX*	Required	Inked stamp or photocopiable embosser	Circular 2" diameter max. or rectangular 1" by 2 ½" max. w/serrated or milled edge border surrounding: "Notary Public" and "State of Texas" appearing around a star of 5 points, Notary's name, comm. exp. date

Table 5 — Journal and Seal Requirements			
State	**Journal**	**Seal**	**Seal Shape/Content**
UT*	Recommended	Purple-inked stamp (embosser only allowed as add-on)	Rectangular, 1" by 2 ½" max. w/Notary's name, "Notary Public", "State of Utah", "My commission expires on (date)", comm. no., Utah Great Seal
VA*	Only for electronic notarial acts	Inked stamp or photocopiable embosser	Notary's name, "Notary Public", "Commonwealth of Virginia", "My commission expires (date)", registration no.
Virgin Islands, U.S.	Required	Embosser (inking stamp only allowed as add-on)	Notary's name, "Notary Public", comm. exp. date, judicial division of Notary's residence, "U.S. Virgin Islands" or "USVI"
VT	Recommended	Optional	No specifications are provided by state
WA*	Recommended	Inked stamp or photocopiable embosser	Min. 8 pt. font; circular 1 $^{5}/_{8}$" min. diameter, rectangular min. 1" by 1 $^{5}/_{8}$"; Notary's name, "State of Washington", "Notary Public", appt. exp. date (Prohibited: Washington Great Seal)
WI	Recommended	Inked rubber stamp or embosser	Only the following words: Notary's name, "Notary Public", "State of Wisconsin"
WV	Recommended	Inked rubber stamp (embosser only allowed as add-on)	Rectangular 1" by 2 ½" max. w/serrated or milled edge border; "Official Seal", "Notary Public", "State of West Virginia", Notary's name, business name if bus. address used, bus. or residence address, "My commission expires (date)" (Optional: W.Va. Great Seal)

Table 5 — Journal and Seal Requirements			
State	**Journal**	**Seal**	**Seal Shape/Content**
WY	Recommended	Inked stamp or photocopiable embosser	Rectangular ¾" by 2 ½" max. or circular 2" max. diameter w/serrated or milled edge border; Notary's name, "Notary Public", Name of county of Notary's residence, "Wyoming" (Optional: comm. exp. date)

* A complete *Notary Law Primer* is published for this state by the National Notary Association. Each such *Primer* is devoted exclusively to an in-depth examination of the statutes, regulations, rulings, directives and customs governing Notaries in the one state.

** In Hawaii, to prevent fraud, the Notary must stamp a "Certification Statement" close by the jurat or acknowledgment wording, then fill out, sign and date this statement, which includes: the Notary's printed name and official stamp or seal, the judicial district venue, and the document's date, description and number of pages. Thus, the Notary's stamp or seal may have to be affixed twice if all the above information is not included in the jurat or acknowledgment wording.

*** In Illinois, due to a statutory program in effect from June 1, 2009, to July 1, 2018, any Illinois Notary must create a "Notarial Record" for conveyances of certain types of residential real property in Cook County. This record, which includes the grantor's thumbprint, is not retained by the Notary but surrendered within 14 days to the Notary's employer or to the Cook County Recorder of Deeds. See Illinois Public Act 988 of 2008 for details.

SPECIAL CIRCUMSTANCES

Signature by Mark

Mark Serves as Signature. A person who cannot sign his or her name because of illiteracy or a physical disability may instead affix a mark — an "X" for example — as a legal signature, as long as there are witnesses to the making of the mark.

Number of Witnesses. State laws vary, but generally, in order for a mark to be notarized, two impartial witnesses in addition to the Notary must view the affixing of the mark. Both witnesses should sign the document (e.g., "John Q. Smith, Witness") and the Notary's journal.

Signature by Mark Certificate. A mark is considered a signature under law, as long as it is properly witnessed. Thus, the Notary uses a standard acknowledgment or jurat certificate — though a few states do dictate or recommend specially adapted certificates for signings by mark, including Connecticut and Florida.

Signature by Proxy

State Laws Vary. In cases where a signer cannot even make a mark, some other arrangement may have to be made. Often, a guardian, also called a conservator, will be appointed by a court to handle the affairs of persons unable to sign or otherwise act on their own behalves.

The Notary does not have the authority to authorize or direct a disabled person to sign using extraordinary procedures (e.g., a pen held in the mouth). Only the person's attorney or another individual officially appointed to look after the person's legal affairs can sanction such procedures.

There are absolutely no circumstances wherein Notaries may allow another person to guide an individual's hand to "sign" a document. The signer may receive no assistance in making the signature or mark.

In a few states, Notaries have the authority to sign the name of a person who is unable to sign or make a mark, or to witness such a signing by a third party. The disabled person must be competent, must personally appear before the Notary and must orally direct the Notary or a third party in the presence of the Notary to sign by proxy. In some states, a certificate of disability signed by the disabled person's physician must also accompany the document. This procedure helps disabled signers handle their affairs.

Impaired Communication Signers

Blind Signer. A prudent Notary will not notarize for a blind person without first reading the document to the person. Indeed, in a few states — including Florida and Indiana — this is a requirement of statute. To avoid the unauthorized practice of law, the Notary must not attempt to explain the document. The reading should be verbatim.

Hearing- and Speech-Impaired Signers. These signers must be able to communicate their willingness and awareness to you and, in the case of a jurat, to indicate compliance with the oath or affirmation.

Often, written notes, gestures or any combination of these, will help you communicate with most hearing- or speech-impaired signers

Notarizing for Minors

Under Age of Majority. Generally, persons must reach the age of majority before they can handle their own legal affairs and sign contracts and other legal documents for themselves. In all but three states, the age of majority is 18. In Alabama, the age of majority is 19 for unmarried, but 18 for married; in Mississippi, it is 21; in Nebraska it is 19. Normally, natural guardians (parents) or court-appointed guardians will sign on a minor's behalf. In certain cases, minors may lawfully sign documents and have their signatures notarized — emancipated minors, minors engaged in business transactions or minors serving as court witnesses, for example.

Include Age Next to Signature. When notarizing for a minor, you should ask the young signer to write his or her age next to the signature to alert any person relying on the document that the signer is a minor. You are not required to verify the minor signer's age.

Identification. The method for identifying a minor is the same as that for an adult. However, determining the identity of a minor can be a problem, because young people often do not possess acceptable identification documents such as driver's licenses or passports.

If the minor does not have an acceptable ID, then the other trustworthy methods of identifying acknowledgers must be used, either your personal knowledge of the minor's identity or the oath of a credible identifying witness — or witnesses — who can identify the minor. (See "Credible Identifying Witness(es)," pages 52–53)

Authentication

Documents Sent to Other Nations. Documents you notarize that are sent to other nations usually are required to bear proof that your signature and seal are genuine and that you had authority to act at the time of notarization. This process of proving the genuineness of an official signature and seal is called authentication or legalization.

The proof is in the form of an authenticating certificate attached to the notarized document by the local county office where your oath is on file and/or by the state Notary-commissioning authority (e.g., Secretary of State). These certificates are known by different names: certificates of authority, certificates of capacity, certificates of authenticity, certificates of prothonotary, and "flags."

Chain Certification. When a notarized document is to be sent out of the United States, a "chain certification" process may be necessary, and additional certificates of authority may have to be obtained from a foreign consulate located in this country, from the U.S. Department of State in Washington, D.C. and from a ministry of foreign affairs in the particular foreign nation.

Apostilles and Hague Convention. Fortunately, over 100 nations, including the United States, subscribe to a treaty that simplifies authentication of notarized documents exchanged between any of the nations. The official name of this treaty, promulgated by the prestigious Hague Conference starting October 5, 1961, is *The Hague Convention Abolishing the Requirement of Legalization for Foreign Public Documents*. (For a list of the subscribing countries, see "Hague Convention Nations," pages 139–141.)

Under this Hague Convention, only one authenticating certificate, called an *apostille*, is necessary to ensure acceptance of a Notary's signature and seal abroad. (*Apostille* means "notation" in French.)

In most states, *apostilles* for notarial acts are issued by the state Notary regulating or commissioning authority.

Advertising

False or Misleading Advertising. Many states have laws prohibiting Notaries from using false or misleading advertising to misrepresent the authority, rights, and privileges of a Notary. For example, a Notary who represents himself to be an immigration expert and who leads clients to believe he has powers beyond those bestowed by law may be guilty of false advertising.

Translation of 'Notary Public.' Some state laws specifically prohibit use of non-English variations of the term "Notary Public" — such as the Spanish *notario publico* — because such foreign officials essentially are attorneys. In addition, these laws usually require any non-English-language ads for notarial services to contain a statement that the Notary is not an attorney, as well as a list of the statutory notarial fees in English and the foreign language.

Foreign Languages

Foreign-Language Documents. Ideally, documents in foreign languages should be referred to Notaries who read and write those languages. If not available in ethnic neighborhoods, bilingual Notaries may often be found in foreign consulates.

States generally do not expressly prohibit their Notaries from notarizing non-English documents, as long as the notarial certificate is in English or in a language the Notary can read.

There are, however, potential difficulties with documents written in a language the Notary cannot read: blatant fraud might go undetected and determining the nature of the document for a journal entry might be impossible. There are also problems when signatures are affixed using letters or characters other than used in the English alphabet.

Foreign-Speaking Signers. Ideally, there should be direct communication between the Notary and document signer, whether in English or any other language. It can be risky for a Notary to rely on an intermediary or interpreter to be assured that a signer is willing, aware, and has the identity claimed. Even so, Arizona is one state whose law allows a translator to mediate between signer and Notary. One clear danger of relying on a translator or interpreter is the possibility that this individual may have a motive for misrepresenting the document or transaction to the signer and/or the Notary.

Immigration

Do Not Give Advice. Non-attorney Notaries may never advise others on the subject of immigration or help others prepare immigration documents — especially not for a fee. Notaries who offer immigration advice to others may be prosecuted for the unauthorized practice of law.

However, Notaries who are "accredited representatives" approved by the Board of Immigration Appeals may assist immigrants with their paperwork, provided they are employed by a specific nonprofit religious, charitable, social service or other similar organization.

Common Documents. Certain immigration documents may be notarized. Some affidavits issued or accepted by the United States Citizenship and Immigration Services (USCIS) are notarized, with the "Affidavit of Support" (Form I-134/I-864) being the most common.

Documents not issued by USCIS are often notarized and submitted in support of an immigration petition. These include translator's declarations, statements from employers and banks, and affidavits of relationship.

If there appears to be no room for a Notary seal on a document issued by USCIS, federal officials advise that the seal may be affixed over boilerplate text (standard printed wording) in the documentation — but never over signatures and other handwriting.

Naturalization Certificates. A Notary may be in violation of federal law if he or she makes a typewritten, photostatic, or any other copy of a Certificate of Naturalization or notarizes it (U.S. Penal Code, Section 75 and U.S. Code, Title 18, Section 137).

Wills

Do Not Offer Advice. Often, people attempt to draw up wills without benefit of legal counsel and then bring these homemade testaments to a Notary to have them "legalized," expecting the Notary to know how to proceed. In advising or assisting such persons, the Notary risks prosecution for the unauthorized practice of law; and the Notary's ill-informed advice may do considerable damage to the affairs of the signer.

Wills are highly sensitive documents, the format of which is dictated by strict laws. The slightest deviation from these laws can nullify a will. In some cases, holographic (handwritten) wills have actually been voided by notarization.

May Notarize Will. A document presented to a Notary as a will may be notarized, but there should be clear instructions and all needed notarial forms should be provided. If the signer of the will (testator) is seeking guidance from the Notary on how to proceed, the Notary should not get involved.

Living Wills. Advanced directives for health care, popularly called living wills, are not actually wills. They are written statements of a signer's wishes concerning medical treatment in the event the signer has an illness or injury and is unable to give instructions on his or her own behalf. Such advanced directives may be notarized.

MISCONDUCT

State Laws Vary. Notary laws differ markedly from state to

state in defining notarial misconduct. Some states, for instance, prescribe stiff criminal penalties for mishandling a Notary journal, while others do not even require Notaries to keep journals. (Of course, wise Notaries in every state keep journals, even if not required to do so by law.)

There are two major forms of notarial misconduct that every state prohibits: false certificates and the unauthorized practice of law.

False Certificates

In every state, it is a criminal offense for a Notary knowingly to make false statements in a notarial certificate. Important transactions in commerce and law depend on the truthfulness and accuracy of the Notary's certificate. Making a notarial certificate, the Tennessee Supreme Court said in 1917 in an often-cited ruling, *Figuers v. Fly*, "is an act which must in the nature of things be relied on with confidence by men of business. Those buying or taking security by way of liens on real estate ought not to be required to look with suspicion on such a certificate."

Misstatements in notarial certificates are caused by a failure to understand the notarial duties required by the certificate, by conscious criminal intent or by simple carelessness. Regardless of the cause, such misinformation in an official certificate is unacceptable and constitutes notarial misconduct. Falsehoods or misstatements in notarial certificates most often involve at least one of three matters: the personal appearance of the signer before the Notary, the identity of the signer or the date of the notarial act.

<u>False Personal Appearance</u>. Virtually every certificate completed by a Notary contains a statement that the principal signed or acknowledged signing "before me" or "in my presence." Yet, sometimes misguided Notaries will not require signers to appear before them. They might perform a notarial act merely on familiarity with a signature on a telephone call, or on the unsworn word of a third party.

Such practices are illegal and dangerous. Not only is the Notary potentially guilty of a criminal act in making a false statement about appearance, but there is a strong possibility that the nonappearing person's signature was forged.

<u>False Identity of Signer</u>. Notarial certificates, particularly those for acknowledgments, often indicate how a signer's identity was established to the Notary, whether by personal knowledge or

satisfactory evidence. However, Notaries sometimes will state that a stranger or barely-known acquaintance is "personally known." Or, they might allow an introduction by a third party to suffice as personal knowledge. This is particularly dangerous.

Too often, signers identified to Notaries through casual introduction by friends prove to be imposters. A Notary should only rely on the word of a third party if that individual is personally known to the Notary, disinterested in the transaction and willing to be formally sworn in as a credible identifying witness.

False Date of Notarization. It is not uncommon for a Notary to be asked to falsify the date of a notarial act. A signer, for instance, may have neglected to observe an important deadline. He then may ask the Notary to put an earlier date on a certificate attached to the tardy papers than the actual date of appearance before the Notary. Of course, such falsification by the Notary is improper and illegal.

Other Certificate Errors. There are many other occasions when a Notary might be prompted to falsify information on a certificate. For example, a Notary may have no knowledge that a signer is vice president of a corporation yet be asked to complete a corporate acknowledgment certificate stating the person is "known to me to be vice president." Or, a Notary may fail to administer an oath or affirmation yet complete a jurat certificate stating a document was "subscribed and sworn to before me."

Unauthorized Practice of Law

Do Not Assist Others with Legal Matters. A non-attorney Notary may not give legal advice or accept fees for legal advice. As a ministerial officer, the non-attorney Notary is generally not permitted to assist other persons in drafting, preparing, selecting, completing, or understanding a document or transaction.

You should not fill in blank spaces in the text of a document for other persons, tell others what documents they need, nor how to draft them, nor advise others about the legal sufficiency of a document — and especially not for a fee.

You may, of course, fill in the blanks on the portion of any document containing the notarial certificate. And you may, as a private individual, prepare legal documents that you are personally a party to; but you may not then notarize your signature on these same documents.

Notaries who overstep their authority by advising others on

legal matters may have their commissions revoked and may be prosecuted for the unauthorized practice of law.

Exceptions. In many states, non-attorney Notaries who are specially trained or licensed in a particular field (e.g., real estate, insurance, escrow) may advise others about documents in that field, but in no other! In addition, trained paralegals under the supervision of an attorney may advise others about documents in routine legal matters.

ELECTRONIC NOTARIZATIONS

Statutory Authority

The explosive growth of electronic commerce has produced a need for Notaries to witness electronic transactions, just as they have witnessed paper transactions for centuries. While the tools for creating and signing documents may be different, the impartial witnessing services of a Notary remain the same and are as important as ever. Any Notary wanting to learn the basics of electronic notarization should be familiar with the following:.

UETA. The Uniform Electronic Transactions Act (UETA), is a uniform law governing electronic transactions. It was created by the National Conference of Commissioners on Uniform State Laws (also called the Uniform Law Commission) to assist state lawmakers in updating their statutes. Since 1999, UETA has been adopted by nearly every U.S. state and the District of Columbia.

Electronic Transactions Legal. The UETA declares that electronic documents and electronic signatures have the same legal effect as paper documents and pen-and-ink signatures. Significantly, UETA states that a transaction cannot be denied legal effect or rejected because it is in electronic form or because electronic means — such as computer hardware, software and electronic signatures — were used in its creation and execution. Further, the UETA says that if a law requires a transaction to be in writing, an electronic document satisfies the law. However, use of electronic documents and signatures is voluntary and no one is required to use them if they prefer paper and pens.

Electronic Notarizations Legal. The UETA expressly authorizes Notaries to use electronic signatures in signing electronic documents if all other information required to be included — for example, the Notary's name, the title "Notary Public" and commission expiration date — is "attached to or logically associated" with the electronic record or signature.

Technological Neutrality. An important principle of the UETA is "technological neutrality." The UETA does not specify or endorse a particular technology for creating, signing, transmitting and storing electronic records nor for affixing electronic signatures. Instead, the parties involved in a transaction simply must agree upon the technology used to sign a document electronically.

Electronic Signatures. A paper document is signed with pen and ink, but an electronic record may be "signed" and authenticated with an electronic signature using any available technology agreed upon by the participants. The UETA defines an electronic signature as an electronic sound, symbol or process executed by a person with the intent to sign an electronic document.

Examples of electronic signatures, with varying levels of security, include:

- A typed name, such as one on the signature line of an electronic document or at the bottom of an email;
- A "click wrap" signature created when a signer clicks an "I accept" or "Click to Sign" button in a software application or on a website, such as when purchasing items online with a credit card;
- A scanned image of a handwritten signature "pasted" into an electronic document;
- A handwritten signature made by using an electronic signature pad or device;
- A voice print, based on the unique physical configuration of the speaker's mouth and throat, which expresses the vocal sample as a mathematical formula;
- A voice message left by telephone;
- A Personal Identification Number (PIN), such as those used

at a bank ATM;

- A telephone prompt or code entered using the dial pad of a touch-tone phone;
- A digital signature affixed by applying cryptographic methods.

Attribution and Security Procedure. Another critically important legal consideration of any electronic signature is attribution. The term attribution describes the process of determining that a signature is the act of a given person. Knowing just who actually signed an electronic document is a fundamental concern. The UETA allows parties executing an electronic transaction to use a "security procedure" to determine the person to which the electronic signature is attributable and to detect changes or errors in the signed record. A security procedure can use technological means — including algorithms or other codes, identifying words or numbers, encryption, callback or other procedures. In addition, a security procedure can use non-technological means. An electronic notarial act qualifies as a security procedure for proving attribution of an electronic signature.

Intent. Another important legal consideration of any signature is intent. Regardless of the actual technology used to create an electronic signature, the party using the technology must adopt it with the intent to sign the electronic document. Determining the signer's intent is one of the key purposes of electronic notarization and the reason signers of electronic documents must appear in person before the Notary for any eNotarization.

Electronic Recording. The Uniform Real Property Electronic Recording Act (URPERA), permits county recorders to accept electronic real property electronic real property records using an electronic signature. The exact rules for recording electronic real estate documents vary from state to state. ■

Test Your Knowledge

This practice quiz is designed to test your knowledge of the basic concepts of notarization. You will find the correct answers to all exam questions on pages 94–95.

Instructions. Work through the exam without looking at the answers, then check your responses and note where you need additional study.

Careful review of this *Primer* will produce the answers.

A perfect score on this quiz is 100 points. The quiz is structured as follows:

- Twenty true/false questions worth one point each
- Five multiple-choice questions worth four points each
- Five fill-in-the-blank questions worth four points each
- Five essay questions worth eight points each

To complete the quiz, you will need a pen or pencil and a separate sheet of paper for your answers to the essay questions.

True/False. For the following statements, answer true or false. Each correct answer is worth one point.

1. Notaries may act only in the county where they are appointed and reside. True or false?

2. It may be difficult to establish a minor's identity because of the lack of adequate ID. True or false?

3. Notaries are commissioned only to serve the customers of their employers. True or false?

4. Notaries must keep a photocopy of every document notarized. True or false?

5. Any notarial certificate may be properly referred to as a jurat. True or false?

6. Notaries can withhold their services if they believe a signer is incompetent and unable to understand a document. True or false?

7. A journal of notarial acts with loose-leaf pages is an excellent way to record a Notary's acts. True or false?

8. The letters "L.S." on a notarial certificate stand for the Latin words *locus sigilli*, which mean "location of the seal." True or false?

9. Holographic wills must be notarized to be valid. True or false?

10. Upon request, it is the Notary's duty to draft powers of attorney, mortgages and deeds. True or false?

11. A Notary may notarize the other signature on a document co-signed by the Notary. True or false?

12. A signer who is unable to write may sign by mark and have the mark notarized if it is witnessed by two other persons. True or false?

13. The Notary need not reimburse the surety company for bond funds paid out to a person financially harmed by the Notary's actions. True or false?

14. After the letters "S.S." on a notarial certificate, the Notary must write his or her Social Security number. True or false?

15. A Notary's stamp and journal belong to the Notary's employer if the employer paid for them. True or false?

16. An acknowledgment certificate may be adapted by the Notary for jurats or proofs of execution by a subscribing witness. True or false?

17. An affirmation is the legal equivalent of an oath, but makes no reference to a Supreme Being. True or false?

18. A Notary employed by a private employer may charge an additional fee for a notarization that requires an excessive amount of time. True or false?

19. Personal appearance includes recognizing a voice over a phone or from the next room. True or false?

20. A Notary may offer testimonials using the "Notary Public" title. True or false?

Multiple Choice. Choose the one best answer to each question. Each correct answer is worth four points.

1. A Notary has no disqualifying interest when acting as which of the following?
   a. A co-borrower on a set of loan documents
   b. A real estate agent selling the signer a condominium
   c. A salaried employee of the signer's company

2. Of the following, which is not one of the five steps of proper notarization?
   a. Identify the signer and screen for willingness and awareness
   b. Make and keep a copy of the document you are notarizing
   c. Review the document for completeness and any obvious frauds

3. Where may an *apostille* be obtained?
   a. Only from the office of the Hague Convention
   b. Only from the office of the Notary's regulating authority
   c. Only from the office of the U.S. Attorney General

4. "Satisfactory evidence" of identity usually means reliance on which of the following?
   a. On personal knowledge only
   b. On ID cards only
   c. On ID cards or credible witnesses

5. In states that empower Notaries to certify copies, a Notary may do which of the following?
   a. Certify a copy of a college diploma
   b. Certify copies of a real property deed
   c. Certify a copy of a foreign birth certificate

Fill in the Blank. Write in the word or phrase that best completes each sentence. Each correct answer is worth four points.

1. The Notary and the ____________ for the Notary's bond are liable for the Notary's neglect and misconduct.

2. A solemn, spoken pledge that is not an affirmation is called a(n) ____________.

3. A trustworthy ID card should at the least contain a(n) ____________ of its bearer.

4. A copy certification attests that the reproduction is ____________ and ____________.

5. Wills written entirely in the testator's own handwriting are called ____________.

Essay. Reply to each question or statement with a short paragraph. Each complete and correct response is worth eight points.

1. Discuss the distinctions between a Notary bond and Notary errors and omissions insurance.

2. How does a proof of execution by a subscribing witness work?

3. What is an *apostille* and when is it used?

4. Why should a Notary always complete the journal entry before filling out a notarial certificate?

5. Outline the differences between an acknowledgment certificate and a jurat.

Test Answers

True/False. 1. F; 2. T; 3. F; 4. F; 5. F; 6. T; 7. F; 8. T; 9. F; 10. F; 11. F; 12. T; 13. F; 14. F; 15. F; 16. F; 17. T; 18. F; 19. F; 20. F

Multiple Choice. 1. c; 2. b; 3. b; 4. c; 5. a

Fill in the Blank. 1. surety; 2. oath; 3. photograph; 4. true, complete; 5. holographic

Essay. Responses should include the basic information in the paragraphs below.

1. A Notary bond, usually obtained through a state-licensed surety company, provides protection for the public in case of the Notary's negligence or intentional misconduct. Up to the cash limit of the bond, the surety agrees to pay damages to anyone who suffers a loss because of the Notary's actions; the Notary, however, must then reimburse the surety. Notary errors and omissions insurance, also purchased from a state-licensed company, protects the Notary in case of an unintentional error, up to the policy limit. The Notary does not reimburse the insurance company. A bond is required by law. Errors and omissions insurance is not.

2. A proof of execution by a subscribing witness sometimes is used in lieu of an acknowledgment when a document's principal signer is unavailable to appear before a Notary. A subscribing witness who has seen the principal sign the document or taken the principle's acknowledgment of the signature may present this document to a Notary on the principal's behalf. The witness must sign ("subscribe") his or her name on the document. The witness must be personally known to the Notary and must swear or affirm to the Notary that he or she witnessed the principal sign or acknowledge the document.

3. An *apostille* is a certificate authenticating the signature and stamp or seal of a Notary. It is issued under the provisions of an international treaty, signed by more than 100 nations, called *The Hague Convention Abolishing the Requirement of Legalization for Foreign Public Documents.* For notarized documents exchanged between the subscribing nations, this treaty streamlines the time-consuming authentication process known as "chain-certification," instead allowing one authenticating certificate, the *apostille* (French for "notation") to suffice. *Apostilles* for are issued by your state's Notary-regulating authority.

4. Filling out a journal entry before completing a notarial certificate prevents a signer from leaving before an important record of the notarization is made in the journal. The journal not only protects the public — it also protects the Notary from false accusations of misconduct.

5. An acknowledgment certificate certifies that the signer of the document personally appeared before the Notary on the date and in the county indicated, that the signer's identity was satisfactorily proven to the Notary and that the signer acknowledged having signed freely. A jurat certificate certifies that the signer of the document personally appeared before the Notary on the date and in the county indicated, that the signer's identity was satisfactorily proven to the Notary, that the signer signed the document in the Notary's presence and that the Notary administered an oath or affirmation to the signer.

Tally Your Score

After checking your answers, add up your score. Then look at the grading scale below to determine how you stand.

- 90–100: Excellent!
- 80–89: Good, but some review needed.
- 70–79: Fair. Reread the parts of the *Primer* covering the answers you missed.
- Below 70: Below par. Study the *Primer* thoroughly again. ■

The Notary Public Code of Professional Responsibility

Published as a public service by the National Notary Association for all Notaries and the public they serve.

July, 2009

CONTENTS

INTRODUCTION

Purpose of the *Code*

The Notary Public's key role in lending integrity to important transactions of commerce and law necessitates sound standards for the performance of notarial acts.

While many occupations pose professional and ethical norms for their practitioners, the need for guidelines is particularly acute with persons holding the office of Notary because of their unusual status as both public and private functionaries. In few offices is the practitioner more subject to conflicting pressures. Yet, in few offices are the guiding statutes so scant and inadequate.

The purpose of *The Notary Public Code of Professional Responsibility* is to guide Notaries Public in the United States when statutes, regulations and official directives fall short.

The standards in this *Code* are of two types. The majority are principles, policies and practices that have proven over the years to be effective in helping Notaries perform their primary function of detecting and deterring fraud; in minimizing fraud, these standards also work to reduce the Notary's exposure to lawsuits. The remainder are standards derived from the conviction that a public officer in a democracy must serve all persons equally, without regard to such distinctions as race, nationality, ethnicity, citizenship, religion, politics, lifestyle, age, disability, gender or sexual orientation.

Because the acts of Notaries affect individual rights and property under both civil and criminal law, it is imperative that professional standards for Notaries be widely acknowledged as just, fair and well-developed. To that end, the standards in this *Code* were drafted with input from representatives of occupational fields with a large constituency of Notaries Public. Also contributing were state and local officials who regulate the activities of Notaries, as well as legal, business and surety experts.

Organization of the Code

This *Code of Professional Responsibility* is based upon 10 widely accepted "Guiding Principles" that clarify the multiple roles of the Notary Public in the United States. They are general rules for responsible conduct.

Each Principle in turn embraces particular "Standards of Professional and Ethical Practice" for the Notary. Each Standard works to maximize the public utility of the notarial office, while minimizing the Notary's exposure to liability.

The Standards of Professional and Ethical Practice are exemplified by "Illustrations" posing problematic situations that are common or typical for Notaries. Details are provided to help the reader visualize each situation.

For each Illustration, "The Ethical Imperative" or "The Professional Choice" indicates the course of action best exemplifying the pertinent Guiding Principle and Standard of Professional and Ethical Practice.

The Ethical Imperative identifies an action that, if not taken, would constitute a clear and serious violation of the Notary's fundamental role as an impartial witnessing official, as defined in the Guiding Principles.

The Professional Choice identifies an action that, if not taken, would undermine or lessen the Notary's effectiveness as a fraud-deterring public servant.

The 10 "Commentary" sections supplement the *Code* by explaining the drafters' views, concerns and rationales in shaping important provisions, and by discussing certain pertinent other matters not directly addressed by the *Code*.

Basis of the *Code*

The Guiding Principles and Standards of Professional and Ethical Practice are the distillation of decades of interaction between the National Notary Association and thousands of Notaries from every walk of life and from every state and U.S. jurisdiction. They address the common problems, issues and questions encountered by Notaries, particularly matters of conflicting interest.

The Principles and Standards reflect the conviction that Notaries must operate in a businesslike fashion, basing their actions on proven practices of business and government, and always carefully documenting their official activities.

Statutory Requirements

In some jurisdictions, a particular Standard of Professional and Ethical Practice may already be a requirement of statute, such as the common but not universal legal mandate to keep a record of all notarial acts performed. In most cases, however, the Standards do not carry the force of law. Therefore, throughout the *Code*, the word "shall" does not necessarily denote a legal obligation for the Notary, but it always constitutes a compelling recommendation.

In rare cases, the Standards may contradict provisions in a state's Notary statutes or administrative regulations, particularly when these rules stipulate procedures for disposal of the seal or journal upon termination of the Notary's commission. In these instances, of course, pertinent statutes and regulations must be obeyed by the Notary.

For the overwhelming majority of Notaries, no statute or administrative rule will prevent adherence to any and every Standard of Professional and Ethical Practice in the Code.

Employer Expectations

The Standards frequently will contradict not the provisions of law but the policies, practices or expectations of the Notary's employer. This is often the case when an employer wishes to discriminate between customers and noncustomers by providing or withholding notarial services that the *Code* stipulates should be available to all.

Notaries should understand that the *Code* is a model for preferred conduct and not a gauge of unlawfulness or criminality.

Uses and Benefits of the *Code*

This *Code* may serve as a tool to guide and educate not only Notaries Public, but also lawmakers, public administrators, private employers and any users of notarial services.

It is a moral imperative for progressive change, and a catalyst for improving notarial statutes and conventions in commerce and law.

Widespread implementation of the *Code* will reduce fraud and litigation.

Any Notary's adherence to the *Code*'s Standards brings confidence that he or she is acting in accord with the highest professional and ethical traditions of the notarial office.

Widespread adherence to the Standards by Notaries in the United States will engender heightened respect and recognition for their notarial office in the enterprises of government and business, both in this nation and abroad.

Revision of the *Code*

The Notary Public Code of Professional Responsibility is not intended to be static and unchangeable. Its organization allows the separable Standards to be added, deleted or amended with little or no disruption of other elements in the *Code*.

While the 10 Guiding Principles of the *Code* are sufficiently general to embrace considerable change in the duties and practices of the Notary office without amendment to their current form, it is likely that the *Code*'s 85 Standards may in time need revision or supplement to accommodate technological developments.

Periodic review and revision of the *Code* are intended.

Notary Public Code of Professional Responsibility Guiding Principles

I The Notary shall, as a government officer and public servant, serve all of the public in an honest, fair and unbiased manner.

II The Notary shall act as an impartial witness and not profit or gain from any document or transaction requiring a notarial act, apart from the fee allowed by statute.

III The Notary shall require the presence of each signer and oath-taker in order to carefully screen each for identity and willingness, and to observe that each appears aware of the significance of the transaction requiring a notarial act.

IV The Notary shall not execute a false or incomplete certificate, nor be involved with any document or transaction that the Notary believes is false, deceptive or fraudulent.

V The Notary shall give precedence to the rules of law over the dictates or expectations of any person or entity.

VI The Notary shall act as a ministerial officer and not provide unauthorized advice or services.

VII The Notary shall affix a seal on every notarized document and not allow this universally recognized symbol of office to be used by another or in an endorsement or promotion.

VIII The Notary shall record every notarial act in a bound journal or other secure recording device and safeguard it as an important public record.

IX The Notary shall respect the privacy of each signer and not divulge or use personal or proprietary information disclosed during execution of a notarial act for other than an official purpose.

X The Notary shall seek instruction on notarization, and keep current on the laws, practices and requirements of the notarial office.

GUIDING PRINCIPLE I

The Notary shall, as a government officer and public servant, serve all of the public in an honest, fair and unbiased manner.

Standards of Professional and Ethical Practice

Article A: Refusal to Notarize

I-A-1: Refusal without Due Cause

The Notary shall not refuse to perform a lawful and proper notarial act without due cause.

Illustration: The Notary is asked by a stranger to notarize that person's signature on a document. However, the Notary is hesitant to notarize for any unknown individual because of a presumed increased likelihood of fraud and liability.

The Ethical Imperative: As a public officer and servant, the Notary notarizes the stranger's signature after identifying this individual, if no improprieties are requested or detected.

I-A-2: Refusal for Reasonable Suspicion

The Notary shall refuse to notarize if the Notary has knowledge, or a reasonable suspicion that can be articulated, that the transaction is unlawful or improper.

Illustration: The Notary is asked by a stranger to notarize that person's signature on a document. As proof of identity, the stranger presents a single identification card, a state driver's license. The Notary notices that the photograph on the license is raised from the surface of the card and appears to overlay a state seal and the signature of a DMV official.

The Ethical Imperative: The Notary refuses to notarize the stranger's document, since there is strong evidence that the ID has been tampered with and bears a false photograph, and that the stranger is an impostor.

I-A-3: Undue Cause for Refusal

The Notary shall not refuse to perform a lawful and proper notarial act because of the signer's race, nationality, ethnicity, citizenship, religion, politics, lifestyle, age, disability, gender or sexual orientation, or because of disagreement with the statements or purpose of a lawful document.

Illustration: The Notary is asked by a stranger to notarize that person's signature on a document. While identifying the stranger, the Notary notes that this person is a member of an ethnic minority group. The Notary has heard that most persons in this ethnic group are untrustworthy, through stories that family and friends have told over the years. The Notary hesitates to perform the notarization.

The Ethical Imperative: The Notary notarizes the stranger's document, if no improprieties are requested or detected. Ethnicity here is irrelevant and, by refusing, the Notary may become liable for violating the stranger's civil rights.

I-A-4: Improper Refusal Due to Nonclient Status

The Notary shall not refuse to perform a lawful and proper notarial act solely because the signer is not a client or customer of the Notary or the Notary's employer.

Illustration: The Notary operates a business. A stranger walks in and requests notarization of a document. The Notary is reluctant to take time away from business to notarize for anyone but customers.

The Ethical Imperative: After identifying the stranger, the Notary notarizes the document, if no improprieties are requested or detected. Notaries are commissioned to serve the public at large, not just the patrons of a particular business. While no document signer is justified in demanding that a Notary "drop everything" to perform a notarial act, the Notary should try to accommodate the request for notarial services within a reasonable time. However, for any sudden request that would be particularly time-consuming or disruptive to business (e.g., notarize 100 documents immediately), it is reasonable for the Notary to reschedule the services to a more convenient time or to refer the signer to another nearby Notary available to perform the acts at once. Accommodating the public's need for notarial services is paramount for the publicly commissioned Notary.

Article B: Fees

I-B-1: Improper Assessment of Fee

The Notary shall not base the charging or waiving of a fee for performing a notarial act, or the amount of the fee, on the signer's race, nationality, ethnicity, citizenship, religion, politics, lifestyle, age, disability, gender or sexual orientation, or on agreement or disagreement with the statements or purpose of a lawful document.

Illustration: The Notary is asked by a stranger to notarize that person's signature on an affidavit for a ballot initiative the Notary opposes. The Notary is inclined to "punish" this proponent of the initiative by charging for the notarization, even though the Notary has never before charged for notarizing.

The Ethical Imperative: The Notary notarizes the stranger's affidavit without charging a fee. If it has been a consistent policy not to charge for performing notarial acts, the ethical Notary will not assess a fee as a punitive measure against a political opponent. The publicly commissioned Notary must strive to serve the public evenhandedly; thus, the best policy is for all to be charged the same, or for none to be charged. However, the Notary may waive the fee for ill or impoverished persons or for other charitable or pro bono causes.

I-B-2: Improper Assessment Due to Nonclient Status

The Notary shall not base the charging or waiving of a fee for performing a notarial act, or the amount of the fee, on whether the signer is a client or nonclient, or a customer or noncustomer, of the Notary or the Notary's employer.

Illustration: The Notary operates a business. A stranger walks in and requests notarization of a document. The Notary performs the notarization but wants to discourage future notarial services for noncustomers that take time away from business. Though never before charging for notarizations, the Notary ponders whether to charge the stranger and to impose a policy of charging noncustomers but not charging regular customers for notarial services.

The Ethical Imperative: The Notary does not charge the stranger for the notarization. Because Notaries are commissioned to serve the public evenhandedly, the ethical Notary does not "punish" persons who do not patronize a particular business by charging a fee for notarial services that are offered free to patrons of the same business. All should be charged the same, or none should be charged.

Article C: Dignity of Office

I-C-1: Dignity Befitting Public Office The Notary shall conduct himself or herself with a dignity befitting a public officer and in a manner that does not bring disrepute or discredit upon the notarial office.

Illustration: The Notary is employed in an office with one other Notary, both notarizing affidavits for coworkers. Each affidavit requires administration of an oath to the affiant. The Notary has heard the colleague say to affiants at the start of an oath, "I know this is stupid, but will you please raise your right hand..."; jokingly, the colleague may also have the signer "swear" by placing a hand on a magazine. The Notary considers whether to be similarly flippant about notarial duties in order to fit in better with coworkers.

The Ethical Imperative: The Notary refrains from adopting the officemate's attitude toward notarization. The Notary cautions the colleague that such improprieties undermine the effectiveness of the notarial act, discredit the office of Notary and may jeopardize or invalidate the document. The Notary decides to report any further such improper liberties with official duties to a supervisor and, if the actions persist, to the state Notary-commissioning authority.

Article D: Advertising and Endorsement

I-D-1: Undignified Advertisement

The Notary shall not advertise notarial services in an undignified or excessively commercial manner.

Illustration: The Notary advertises in the telephone book a willingness to notarize "Anytime, Anywhere." To compete against other traveling Notaries, the Notary considers running a new ad that would state, "I Will Not Be Undersold!" and, "I'm Crazy — I'll Go Anywhere At Any Hour!"

The Ethical Imperative: The Notary does not place the new advertisement, since it treats the public office of Notary in both an undignified and an excessively commercial manner.

I-D-2: Misrepresentation

The Notary shall not misrepresent the notarial office; claim or advertise powers, authority, advantages or rights that the office does not give; nor use language that is likely to mislead non-natives of the United States about the powers of the office.

Illustration: The Notary owns a shop in an area with a large concentration of Latin-American immigrants. The Notary wants to put a sign in the shop window to advertise notarial services, but ponders whether it should read "Notary" or "Notario."

The Ethical Imperative: The Notary does not advertise using the Spanish term Notario Publico or Notaria Publica because this is the title of an attorney-like officer in Latin nations and it may mislead immigrants into thinking that U.S. Notaries have the same powers and are entitled to the same fees.

I-D-3: Endorsement Improper

The Notary shall not use or allow use of the Notary's seal or title ("Notary Public") to endorse, extol or denigrate a product, service, program, proposal, individual, candidate, organization or contest, or to corroborate or disprove claims about them.

Illustration: The Notary is a volunteer for a charity that will raffle off a new car to raise funds. So that the raffle is perceived as honest and aboveboard, the president of the charity wants to advertise that the contest will be "Notary-Supervised and Guaranteed," using the name of the Notary.

The Ethical Imperative: The Notary does not allow notarial office to be used to lend seeming integrity or credibility to a contest, regardless of the nobility of its cause. Guaranteeing and certifying the integrity of contests is not an authorized notarial act. Further, the Notary should not notarize any document (e.g., an affidavit signed by the president of the charity) with knowledge that the notarial seal or title will be used in a solicitation or endorsement, since some persons associate any involvement by a Notary with official government certification.

Article E: Ability and Availability to Serve

I-E-1: Resignation if Impaired

The Notary shall resign from office if any permanent change in the Notary's physical status would prevent or significantly impair the proper performance of notarial duties.

Illustration: The Notary is a retiree whose eyesight has deteriorated considerably in recent years. Even with glasses, the Notary is only able to read if the letters are unusually large and bold; distinguishing faces is very difficult.

The Ethical Imperative: The Notary must immediately resign the commission, since such poor eyesight prevents the careful scrutinizing of ID cards and faces required for proper performance of notarial duties and protection of the public from document fraud. Any physical condition that prevents a Notary from directly and personally gleaning information about a signer's identity and about the circumstances of a particular notarization, without reliance on an assistant or intermediary to make such determinations, is a disqualifying one.

I-E-2: Refusal for Lack of Knowledge

The Notary shall decline to notarize if the Notary does not feel sufficiently knowledgeable or competent to perform properly any requested notarial act.

Illustration: The Notary is asked to execute a protest by a stranger who presents a technically-worded notarial form. When the Notary admits to having no idea how to complete the form, the stranger says, "Don't worry, I'll walk you through it."

The Ethical Imperative: The Notary declines to notarize without the knowledge to proceed competently and confidently. Only a specially trained or experienced Notary who is familiar with pertinent provisions of the Uniform Commercial Code should undertake the technically complex notarial act of protest.

I-E-3: Reporting Pertinent Change

The Notary shall report to the commissioning agency any pertinent change in personal status — including change of name or address, conviction of a felony, or adjudicated liability in a lawsuit involving a notarial act — affecting the Notary's availability to the public and the repute of the Notary as a person of integrity.

Illustration: The Notary is planning a permanent move to live and work in another state. There are two years remaining in the commission term.

The Ethical Imperative: The Notary reports the move to the state Notary-commissioning authority and resigns the commission. State officials must know the whereabouts of all Notaries and be kept apprised of their availability to serve the state's citizenry.

GUIDING PRINCIPLE II

The Notary shall act as an impartial witness and not profit or gain from any document or transaction requiring a notarial act, apart from the fee allowed by statute.

Standards of Professional and Ethical Practice

Article A: Improper Gain

II-A-1: Actual or Potential Gain Improper

The Notary shall decline to notarize in any transaction that would result, directly or indirectly, in any actual or potential gain or advantage for the Notary, financial or otherwise, apart from the fee for performing a notarial act allowed by statute.

Illustration: The Notary sells machinery and related maintenance contracts, which must be notarized. The Notary's receipt of a sales commission depends on the employer's receipt of a notarized contract signed by the customer. After convincing a customer to purchase a contract, the Notary then often quickly notarizes the customer's signature out of fear that the person's mind will change, even though there usually are other employees available who could notarize.

The Ethical Imperative: The Notary decides not to notarize while profiting financially from a transaction, letting an uninvolved person perform the required notarization. The roles of impartial witness and advocate are incompatible. Notaries should never take actions to deter signers from changing their minds; one of the major purposes of notarization is to ensure that signers are acting freely.

II-A-2: Commission or Fee Improper

The Notary shall not notarize for a client or customer who will pay the Notary a commission or fee for the resulting transaction, apart from the fee for performing a notarial act allowed by statute.

Illustration: The Notary is an attorney preparing documents for an ailing client who will pay a fee for the task. Several of the documents require notarization. Since the attorney must go to the home of the bedridden client to secure the needed signatures, there will be no paralegal or secretary on hand to notarize the papers. The attorney considers the propriety of serving as Notary in this situation.

The Ethical Imperative: The Notary decides not to notarize, lest it be falsely alleged that a financial interest in the documents resulted in undue influence or the overlooking of lack of mental capacity. Instead, the attorney arranges to have a truly impartial Notary visit the client's home to notarize the documents.

Article B: Improper Personal Interest

II-B-1: Notarization of Own Signature Improper

The Notary shall not notarize his or her own signature.

Illustration: The Notary is about to sign an insurance affidavit of loss for a fire in the Notary's house. At the end of the document is a jurat with blank space for a Notary's signature and seal. The Notary ponders whether the insurance company will mind or even notice if the affiant and the Notary are the same person.

The Ethical Imperative: The Notary finds another person to notarize the signature. There is no greater breach of the Notary's requisite role as impartial witness than "notarizing" one's own signature. Indeed, the very concept of "notarizing for oneself" is as much a contradiction in terms as "marrying oneself" or "pardoning oneself."

II-B-2: Notarization of Cosignature Improper

The Notary shall not notarize a signature on a document that the Notary has cosigned.

Illustration: The Notary and the Notary's business partner need to have their signatures notarized on a document. Aware that notarizing one's own signature is improper, the Notary ponders whether to notarize the partner's signature.

The Ethical Imperative: The Notary does not notarize the partner's signature because, as a cosigner, the Notary has an obvious personal interest in the document that is incompatible with a requisite impartial role. The two partners arrange to have another Notary notarize the two signatures.

II-B-3: Notarization of Document Naming Notary Improper

The Notary shall not notarize a document that bears the name of the Notary or of a close relative, as defined below in Standard II-B-5.

Illustration: The Notary is asked by a friend to be the named agent on a document giving the Notary authority to make health care decisions for the friend in case of severe illness. The friend then asks the Notary to notarize this same document.

The Ethical Imperative: The Notary declines to notarize because, being named in the document as the individual who is thereby given certain life-and-death decision-making powers, the Notary has an obvious personal interest in it that is incompatible with a requisite impartial role.

II-B-4: Notarization of Personal Document Improper

The Notary shall not notarize a document that will affect or involve the Notary's personal affairs.

Illustration: The Notary is informed by the Notary's roommate that the roommate will receive the gift of a condominium from a grandmother. Promising that the Notary may live in one of the bedrooms rent-free, the roommate asks the Notary to visit the grandmother to notarize her signature on the gift-deed.

The Ethical Imperative: The Notary declines to notarize because the Notary will personally benefit from the transaction. Such a beneficial financial impact on one's personal affairs is incompatible with the Notary's requisite impartial role. The roommates arrange to have an uninvolved Notary visit the grandmother.

II-B-5: Notarization for Close Relative Improper

The Notary shall decline to notarize the signature of a close relative or family member, particularly a spouse, parent, grandparent, sibling, son, daughter or grandchild of the Notary, or a stepchild, stepsibling, stepparent, stepgrandparent or stepgrandchild of the Notary.

Illustration: The Notary is asked by the Notary's father to notarize a document that specifies desired medical treatment in the event the father becomes unable to make such decisions. The Notary is not mentioned in the document.

The Ethical Imperative: The Notary declines to notarize and asks the father to have a Notary who is unrelated and truly disinterested notarize the document. It will thereby be rendered less open to challenge and the charge that undue influence was exerted on the signer by a family member.

Article C: Avoiding Appearance of Partiality

II-C-1: Compromise of Impartiality

The Notary shall decline to notarize in any transaction that would impugn, compromise or call into question the Notary's impartiality or propriety, or has the potential for doing so.

Illustration: The Notary is asked by the godmother of the Notary's children to notarize a document that will create a trust fund to benefit the children. The godmother will endow the trust with her own funds. The Notary is not mentioned in the document.

The Ethical Imperative: The Notary declines to notarize, since impartiality and undue influence may otherwise become issues in a transaction that will greatly benefit the Notary's own children. The Notary asks the godmother to have an uninvolved person notarize the document.

Article D: Proper and Improper Influence

II-D-1: Avoidance of Influence in Lawful Transaction

The Notary shall not attempt to influence a person to sign or not sign, to act or not act, nor to proceed or not proceed in any lawful transaction requiring a notarial act that is to be performed by the Notary.

Illustration: The Notary is asked by an acquaintance to notarize that person's signature on documents related to the purchase of a restaurant. Aware of the high failure rate of such businesses, the Notary considers whether to urge the acquaintance to reconsider the decision to purchase.

The Ethical Imperative: The Notary notarizes the documents, if no improprieties are requested or detected. It is not the role of the impartial Notary to argue for or against a signer's participation in a lawful transaction.

II-D-2: Refusing Unlawful Transaction

The Notary shall refuse to participate and shall attempt to influence a person not to sign, not to act or not to proceed in any unlawful transaction requiring a notarial act that is to be performed by the Notary.

Illustration: The Notary is asked by an acquaintance to notarize that person's signature on an affidavit for an immigration petition. The affidavit contains false statements that the Notary knows are fabrications by the signer.

The Ethical Imperative: The Notary refuses to notarize and thereby abet the unlawful act of perjury. The Notary urges the acquaintance not to sign an untruthful affidavit.

Article E: Notarization for Employer

II-E-1: Notarization by Employee Proper

The Notary who is an employee shall be Permitted to notarize for any officer, executive, supervisor, coworker, subordinate, client or customer of the employing organization, as long as the Notary will not gain a commission, bonus or other consideration as a result of the notarial act, other than the regular salary or hourly wage and the statutory notarial fee.

Illustration: The Notary is employed in an office and every day notarizes the signature of a supervisor on dozens of documents. The Notary wonders whether it is proper to be notarizing for the person who supervises one's work and signs one's paycheck.

The Ethical Imperative: As long as the "in-house" Notary receives no special compensation as a result of any notarization and is not asked to notarize improperly, that Notary may notarize company documents.

GUIDING PRINCIPLE III

The Notary shall require the presence of each signer and oath-taker in order to carefully screen each for identity and willingness, and to observe that each appears aware of the significance of the transaction requiring a notarial act.

Standards of Professional and Ethical Practice

Article A: Physical Presence

III-A-1: Insisting That Signer Appear

The Notary shall insist that the signer and any witness identifying the signer be present before the Notary at the time of the notarization.

Illustration: The Notary is telephoned by a client who has just signed and mailed several documents for the Notary to notarize without personal appearance. "You know my signature, so there shouldn't be any problem," the client says over the telephone.

The Ethical Imperative: The Notary declines to perform a "telephone notarization" without the physical presence of the signer, since it would be a clear violation of the law, even though the Notary feels relatively certain about the identity, volition and awareness of the signer.

Article B: Screening for Identity and Willingness

III-B-1: Three Identification Methods

The Notary shall carefully identify each signer through either personal knowledge, at least one reliable identification document bearing a photograph, or the sworn word of a credible witness.

Illustration: The Notary is approached by a friend and a stranger identified by the friend as a business associate. The friend requests notarization of the associate's signature on a document, but is not involved in the transaction. When the Notary asks the associate for identification, the friend becomes indignant that "you won't take my word as my bond."

The Ethical Imperative: The Notary continues to insist either that the associate produce a reliable form of identification bearing a photograph or that the friend be formally sworn in as a credible witness vouching for the associate's identity.

III-B-2: Deterring Undue Influence

The Notary shall not notarize for any person if the Notary has a reasonable belief that can be articulated that the person is being bullied, threatened, intimidated or otherwise unduly influenced into acting against his or her will or interest.

Illustration: The Notary is called to the hospital room of a patient to notarize that person's signature on several documents. The patient appears disinterested in the documents and expresses a desire to be allowed to sleep. Also present is the patient's spouse, who insists that the patient first attend to signing the documents. The spouse places a pen in the patient's hand and directs it to the signature space on one of the documents, but the patient makes no effort to sign.

The Ethical Imperative: The Notary respects the patient's wish to sleep, promising to return later and to notarize if the patient appears alert and willing to sign the documents.

Article C: Screening for Awareness

III-C-1: Awareness Essential in Signer

The Notary shall not notarize for any person if the Notary has a reasonable belief that can be articulated that the person at the moment is not aware of the significance of the transaction requiring a notarial act.

Illustration: The Notary is called to the home of an elderly person to notarize that individual's signature on several documents. The Notary is introduced to the would-be signer by the person's relative. Acting in a childlike manner, the elderly person appears disinterested in the documents. Though the relative urges the Notary to act, the Notary is unable to get a coherent response to simple questions regarding the notarial act (e.g., "Is that your signature, and have you signed this document willingly?").

The Ethical Imperative: The Notary does not notarize the documents, since the person's conduct indicates a strong likelihood that the individual is not at the moment capable of responsible action.

III-C-2: Coherent Communication Necessary

The Notary shall not notarize for any person unable to communicate coherently with the Notary at the time of notarization.

Illustration: The Notary is called to a nursing home to notarize documents for a bedridden patient, whose friend is also present. The patient is awake and sitting up, with both documents signed and resting on a tray table. However, the patient's speech is slurred and the individual is not coherently responsive to the Notary's greeting and questions. The friend urges the Notary to notarize.

The Ethical Imperative: The Notary declines to notarize because, without clear and direct two-way communication with the signer, the Notary cannot be sure of the individual's awareness. The Notary must not rely on an "interpreter" who may have a motive for misrepresenting the signer's condition or intent.

III-C-3: Direct Communication Necessary

The Notary shall not notarize for any person with whom the Notary cannot directly communicate in the same language, regardless of the presence of a third-party interpreter or translator.

Illustration: The Notary is approached by a client and a stranger who does not speak English, but offers a foreign passport as proof of identity. The client says the stranger wants to have a signature notarized on an English-language power of attorney authorizing the client to conduct business on the stranger's behalf. With no knowledge of the stranger's language, the Notary must rely on the client to communicate.

The Ethical Imperative: The Notary declines to notarize for the stranger, since there can be no certainty of this individual's intent or awareness without direct communication. Further, the client has a clear interest in the transaction that compromises reliability as a truthful interpreter. The safest policy would be to direct the two to a Notary who speaks the stranger's language or to the nearest consulate of the stranger's country.

Article D: Qualification of Witnesses

III-D-1: Honesty, Capacity and Disinterest Essential

The Notary shall require any witness identifying a principal signer to be honest, mentally capable and unaffected by the transaction requiring a notarial act.

Illustration: The Notary is asked by a former school classmate to swear that person in as a subscribing witness vouching for the signature of an absent "business associate" on a deed. Over the years, the Notary has developed a poor opinion of the classmate's integrity, having knowledge of a conviction for trafficking in stolen goods.

The Ethical Imperative: The Notary declines to accept the former classmate as a reliable subscribing witness, urging this individual to have the absent business associate appear in person before a Notary.

III-D-2: Oath or Affirmation Necessary for Identifying Witness

The Notary shall administer an oath or affirmation to any witness identifying a principal signer in order to compel truthfulness.

Illustration: The Notary is telephoned by a client who promises to stop by later in the day with a deed to be notarized. The client mentions that the deed requires one witness in addition to the Notary, and asks if a friend may witness the signature on the document before it is brought in.

The Professional Choice: The Notary explains that the client may sign the deed and have the signature witnessed outside of the Notary's presence prior to appearing before the Notary to acknowledge the signature. The Notary also explains that it will not be necessary for the witness to appear and take an oath, since the Notary will positively identify the client based on personal knowledge of identity and not rely on the witness to make the identification.

III-D-3: Personal Knowledge of Identifying Witness Essential

The Notary shall personally know any individual serving as the sole witness identifying a principal signer in the Notary's presence, and the witness shall personally know the principal signer.

in and requests notarization of a document. However, the stranger no longer drives and cannot present a driver's license or other reliable ID card as identification. At that moment, a longtime coworker of the Notary enters and greets the stranger by name. The coworker has known the individual for years.

The Professional Choice: The Notary notarizes the signature of the elderly stranger, who is identified through the vouching under oath of the coworker. The critical chain of personal knowledge exists: the Notary personally knows the identifying witness and the identifying witness personally knows the signer. State law may provide assistance in usefully defining "personal knowledge of identity."

III-D-4: Identifying Witness Must Be Unaffected

The Notary shall disqualify any person from serving as an identifying witness if that individual is named in or affected by the document signed by the principal.

Illustration: The Notary is asked by a married couple to notarize their signatures on a document. The Notary personally knows one of the two as a former college classmate, but has never met the other, who does not drive nor have a driver's license or other photo ID. The couple suggests that the Notary swear in the classmate as a witness to identify the spouse.

The Professional Choice: The Notary agrees to notarize the signature of the spouse who is personally known, but declines to notarize the signature of the unknown spouse, since identification would be based on the word of a witness who is clearly involved in and affected by the transaction. The Notary suggests that the unknown spouse visit a Notary who personally knows that spouse, or rely on a disinterested credible acquaintance who personally knows a Notary to make the identification.

III-D-5: Personal Knowledge of Subscribing Witness Essential

The Notary shall personally know any individual offering to serve as a subscribing witness to identify a principal signer who is not in the Notary's presence.

Illustration: The Notary is asked by a stranger to take a proof of execution for the signature of the stranger's absent spouse. The stranger explains that the spouse was suddenly called out of town on emergency business, but that the stranger saw the spouse sign the document.

The Professional Choice: The Notary declines to allow the stranger to serve as a subscribing witness for a proof of execution because this individual is not personally known to the Notary. Because proofs have a high potential for fraud, Notaries must know well any individual they trust to vouch for an absent signer's identity, volition and awareness.

III-D-6: Subscribing Witness Must Be Unaffected

The Notary shall disqualify any person from serving as a subscribing witness if that individual is named in or affected by the document signed by the absent principal.

Illustration: The Notary is asked by a friend to perform a proof of execution for the signature of the friend's parent on a health care power of attorney naming the friend as attorney in fact. The parent is described as too sick to appear before the Notary.

The Professional Choice: The Notary declines to allow the friend to serve as a subscribing witness for a proof of execution because this individual is named in and affected by the document and the person's credibility as a reliable witness would be compromised.

III-D-7: Two Witnesses to Mark Must Be Disinterested

The Notary shall require that two individuals in addition to the Notary witness the affixation of a mark, and neither witness shall be named in or affected by the marked document.

Illustration: The Notary is called to the bedside of a patient to notarize this person's signature on a power of attorney naming a spouse as attorney in fact. Ill and extremely weak, the patient is only able to affix an "X" rather than a normal signature. The spouse offers to sign as a witness to the mark.

The Professional Choice: The Notary explains that two persons in addition to the Notary must witness the making of the mark. The Notary disqualifies the spouse as a witness, since this individual is both named in and affected by the document. Instead, the spouse finds two neighbors, both of whom present reliable ID cards, to witness the patient's mark.

GUIDING PRINCIPLE IV

The Notary shall not execute a false or incomplete certificate, nor be involved with any document or transaction that the Notary believes is false, deceptive or fraudulent.

Standards of Professional and Ethical Practice

Article A: Certificate Mandatory

IV-A-1: Notarial Wording Required

The Notary shall not notarize any document unless it bears jurat, acknowledgment or other notarial "certificate" wording that specifies what the Notary is attesting.

Illustration: The Notary is asked by a stranger to "certify" an engineering drawing to protect an invention. When the Notary appears perplexed by the request, the stranger says, "Just stamp, date and sign it — that's all I need."

The Ethical Imperative: The Notary declines to "notarize" any document that does not bear notarial certificate language. Merely "stamping, dating and signing" is insufficient because there is no wording to indicate exactly what the Notary's seal and signature are certifying.

Article B: Fraudulent Certificate

IV-B-1: False Statement Improper

The Notary shall not knowingly issue a certificate containing information that is false, deceptive, inaccurate or incomplete.

Illustration: The Notary is asked by a friend to notarize a deed bearing the signatures of the friend and an absent spouse, who "is out of town on business for several days." The acknowledgment form has been prepared beforehand and states that both friend and spouse "personally appeared" before the Notary. The friend explains that the document must be quickly notarized and recorded before the spouse returns because of an escrow deadline.

The Ethical Imperative: The Notary declines to notarize using the prepared notarial certificate, since it falsely states that the spouse was in the Notary's presence. However, the Notary offers to notarize the signature of the friend alone if Permitted to cross out the spouse's name and modify the notarial certificate to reflect that only the friend appeared.

IV-B-2: False Date Improper

The Notary shall not knowingly issue a certificate for a notarial act that indicates a date other than the actual date on which the notarial act was performed.

Illustration: The Notary is asked by a friend to notarize several documents related to charitable contributions. All of the notarial certificates have been prepared for the Notary, who notices that the jurat on one of the documents bears a date in the previous year. When the Notary points this out, the friend explains that a significant financial loss will be suffered unless a contribution is backdated to fall on or before the previous December 31. The friend asks the Notary to "just do a small favor and overlook the minor discrepancy regarding the date."

The Ethical Imperative: The Notary declines to notarize using a certificate with a false date, since it untruthfully states that the notarization was performed on a day on which the friend had not actually appeared.

Article C: Certificate Completion and Attachment

IV-C-1: Completion by Notary Essential

The Notary shall personally prepare or verify all information and insertions on a notarial certificate, and allow no other person to affix the Notary's official signature and seal.

Illustration: The Notary is asked by a stranger to notarize that person's signature on a document. The Notary notices, however, that the document's notarial certificate wording has been filled in beforehand with an incorrect out-of-state venue.

The Professional Choice: Before completing the certificate, the Notary corrects its venue by lining through the inappropriate state and county, then right above printing the state and county in which the notarization is actually being performed. After initialing the venue changes, the Notary completes the certificate.

IV-C-2: Secure Attachment by Notary Essential

The Notary shall take steps in attaching a "loose" notarial certificate to a document that will deter its fraudulent removal and reattachment to an unintended document.

Illustration: The Notary is asked by a stranger to notarize that person's signature on a document that was prepared in another state. However, the document bears preprinted acknowledgment certificate wording that is unacceptable in the Notary's state because it does not detail how the signer was identified. The Notary explains to the stranger that a "loose" certificate bearing acceptable wording will have to be attached. The Notary then completes, signs and seals the certificate, stapling it to the left margin of the document's signature page.

The Professional Choice: To make fraudulent reattachment of the certificate difficult, the Notary writes a brief description of the document on the certificate (e.g., "This certificate is attached to a grant deed dated . . . for property in . . ."). In addition, the Notary embosses the certificate and signature pages together with a seal bearing the Notary's name, writing, "Attached document bears this embossment," on the certificate as well.

IV-C-3: Completion or Attachment by Another Improper

The Notary shall not deliver a signed notarial certificate to another person and trust that person to complete or attach that certificate to a document outside of the Notary's presence.

Illustration: The Notary receives a telephone call from a person for whom eight days earlier the Notary had notarized a deed. Calling from out of state, this individual reports that the Notary neglected to affix a seal imprint on the deed's acknowledgment certificate and that the missing seal has prevented the document from being recorded, thereby "putting an important deal on hold." The caller claims that the Notary's mistake has delayed and possibly endangered a land transaction involving multiple parties and hundreds of thousands of dollars in escrow. The caller asks the Notary to complete and overnight-mail another certificate to replace the defective one. "Since we're being held up by your mistake, you have an obligation to help us get this deal back on track as soon as possible," the caller tells the Notary.

The Ethical Imperative: The Notary declines to complete and mail a new acknowledgment certificate, not trusting an unseen person to attach it to the appropriate document. However, the Notary offers to correct the original certificate by adding the missing seal imprint, if the deed is returned.

Article D: Potentially Fraudulent Documents

IV-D-1: Incomplete Documents Improper

The Notary shall refuse to notarize any document whose text is blank or incomplete.

Illustration: The Notary is asked by a stranger to notarize that person's signature on a document containing blank spaces. "That information isn't available right now and I want to get the notarization out of the way," the stranger says. "It shouldn't make any difference, since you're just certifying my signature, not the terms in the document."

The Professional Choice: The Notary refuses to proceed as asked, explaining to the stranger that the document will be less subject to legal challenge if the signer knows all its terms at the time of notarization.

IV-D-2: Facsimile Signature Improper

The Notary shall refuse to notarize any signature not affixed by hand in pen and ink, unless the law expressly allows otherwise.

Illustration: The Notary works in an office and notarizes several dozen documents every day for an executive. One day, the executive presents a stack of documents for notarization that, instead of being signed by pen, have been stamped with an inked facsimile signature. "I've decided to start using the stamp to save time," the executive tells the Notary.

The Professional Choice: The Notary asks the executive to affix an actual signature on the documents in pen and ink, explaining that the stamped facsimile may not be accepted as a lawful signature.

Article E: Fraudulent Notarization or Transaction

IV-E-1: Improper Notarization

The Notary shall refuse to perform any notarial act that is illegal, dishonest, deceptive, false, improper or in violation of The Ethical Imperatives of this Notary Public Code of Professional Responsibility.

Illustration: The Notary is asked by a client to notarize a document bearing the client's own signature and that of a stranger whom the client introduces as a spouse. The stranger has no documentary identification, claiming to have left it in a car several blocks away. The client grows indignant when the Notary expresses concern about the stranger's lack of IDs and suggests that the person return to the car to get them. The client threatens to do business elsewhere if the Notary does not "trust me enough to do me a small favor."

The Ethical Imperative: The Notary refuses to notarize unless the stranger returns with proper identification, because an introduction by a clearly interested party does not suffice as a reliable identification. It would be illegal and deceptive for the Notary to certify the stranger as personally known or positively identified when this is not actually the case.

IV-E-2: Improper Transaction

The Notary shall refuse to perform any notarial act in connection with a document or transaction that the Notary knows, or has a reasonable suspicion that can be articulated, is illegal, dishonest, deceptive, false or improper.

Illustration: The Notary is asked by an acquaintance to notarize that person's signature on an "affidavit of citizenship" to facilitate travel in a foreign country. The affidavit contains statements that the Notary knows are false.

The Ethical Imperative: The Notary refuses to notarize, explaining to the acquaintance that, having knowledge that statements in the affidavit are false, the Notary has an obligation as a public official not to abet a deception.

IV-E-3: Reporting Illegality

The Notary shall report to appropriate law enforcement or disciplinary authorities any illegality requested, required, proposed or performed that involves a notarial act by the Notary or by any other Notary.

Illustration: The Notary is asked by a stranger to notarize that person's signature on a property deed. The stranger presents a Social Security card and a birth certificate as identification. When the Notary explains that these are inadequate proofs of identity and that a governmentally issued photo-bearing ID such as a driver's license must be presented, the stranger says, "I've lost my driver's license. Will five hundred dollars be enough to expedite this notarization?"

The Ethical Imperative: The Notary refuses to notarize because of the inadequate documentation of identity. Having a strong suspicion that the stranger is an impostor, the Notary reports the encounter to the forgery division of the local police department, providing whatever information the police require.

GUIDING PRINCIPLE V

The Notary shall give precedence to the rules of law over the dictates or expectations of any person or entity.

Standards of Professional and Ethical Practice

Article A: Precedence of Law

V-A-1: Conflict with Dictate or Expectation

The Notary shall obey and give precedence to any pertinent law, regulation or official directive, or any of The Ethical Imperatives of this *Notary Public Code of Professional Responsibility*, when they conflict with the dictates or expectations of an employer, supervisor, client, customer, coworker, associate, partner, friend, relative or any other person or entity.

Illustration: The Notary notarizes daily for executives in a company headquarters. State law requires the Notary to maintain a journal of all notarial acts, including the signature of each document signer. As a convenience to the busy executives, a supervisor directs the Notary to secure the signature of each in the front of the Notary's journal and to have that suffice as the required signature for any future notarial act. The supervisor explains that this will take up less of the executives' time.

The Ethical Imperative: The Notary declines, explaining to the supervisor that state law requires a journal signature from each document signer at the time of notarization; doing so provides physical evidence that the signer actually appeared before the Notary and willingly engaged in the transaction. The Notary further explains that such strict adherence to procedure will render each document less subject to legal challenge, and that failure to comply may cause revocation of the Notary's commission.

V-A-2: Waiving Personal Appearance Improper

The Notary shall not waive the requirement that each signer personally appear before the Notary at the time of notarization at the direction or request of an employer, supervisor, client, customer, coworker, associate, partner, friend, relative or any other person or entity.

Illustration: The Notary is asked by a supervisor to notarize several documents that have been signed and handed to the supervisor by the firm's president, who "will be in important meetings all day and won't have time to be interrupted." All documents bear acknowledgment certificates stating that the signer "personally appeared" before the Notary. The supervisor explains that the Notary may rely on familiarity with the president's signature, having notarized for this executive "hundreds of times before." The supervisor promises that the president will sign the Notary's journal as soon as time allows.

The Ethical Imperative: The Notary refuses to notarize unless the executive is present, as the acknowledgment certificates clearly stipulate and as the law clearly requires. The Notary suggests that the supervisor consider whether proofs of execution might be acceptable substitutes for the acknowledgments, with the supervisor serving as a subscribing witness and declaring under oath that the signatures were acknowledged in the supervisor's presence and are genuine; such proofs, however, would necessitate replacing the acknowledgment forms.

V-A-3: Informal Introduction Improper

The Notary shall not base the identification of any signer on the word of an employer, supervisor, client, customer, coworker, associate, partner, friend, relative or any other person unless the latter is formally sworn in as a credible witness and is not personally a party or beneficiary of the transaction.

Illustration: The Notary is asked by a supervisor to notarize the signature of a client who will be visiting later in the day to sign a contract. The client is a stranger to the Notary. The supervisor directs the Notary to be "as unobtrusive as possible." When the Notary asks what being unobtrusive means, the supervisor says, "It means don't bother the client by asking for ID cards."

The Ethical Imperative: The Notary informs the supervisor that state law requires "satisfactory evidence of identity" for any document signer not personally known. Though the law does not define "satisfactory evidence of identity," it is the Notary's policy to accept only a reliable ID bearing a photograph, or the sworn word of a personally known credible witness who is not involved in the transaction, in lieu of personal knowledge. Knowing the visiting client and not being personally involved in the transaction, the supervisor offers to be sworn in as a credible witness.

Article B: Commission of Employee

V-B-1: Notary Retains Commission

The Notary shall not be required by an employer to surrender or resign the commission upon termination of employment, even if the employer paid for the commission.

Illustration: The Notary informs an employer of the intent to leave in two weeks for another job. The employer says that office policy will require the Notary to hand over the commission certificate and cancel the bond, because the Notary was commissioned and bonded at the company's expense.

The Ethical Imperative: The Notary declines to surrender the commission certificate or resign the commission. Regardless of who paid for the commission, it belongs solely to the Notary, not the employer, and any decision to resign belongs solely to the Notary. In addition, the Notary's surety bond may not unilaterally be cancelled by the Notary or an employer; it must remain in place for the full commission term to protect the public against misconduct by the Notary.

GUIDING PRINCIPLE VI

The Notary shall act as a ministerial officer and not provide unauthorized advice or services.

Standards of Professional and Ethical Practice

Article A: Prescribing Notarial Act

VI-A-1: Selecting Certificate Improper

The Notary who is not an attorney, or a professional duly trained or certified in a pertinent field, shall not determine or prescribe the particular type of notarial act or notarial certificate required in a given transaction.

Illustration: The Notary is asked by a stranger to notarize a letter giving the stranger's friend permission to authorize medical treatment for a child. When the Notary asks the type of notarization needed — jurat or acknowledgment — the stranger says, "You decide for me. I have no idea."

The Ethical Imperative: The Notary shows the language of a standard jurat and a standard acknowledgment certificate, then asks the stranger to decide which is appropriate. If the stranger cannot decide, the Notary must ask this individual to contact either the person or agency directing that the letter be notarized, or the medical facility where the letter would be presented, for further instructions.

Article B: Prescribing or Preparing Document

VI-B-1: Selecting Document Improper

The Notary who is not an attorney, or a professional duly trained or certified in a pertinent field, shall not determine or prescribe the particular type of document required in a given transaction.

Illustration: The Notary is asked by a stranger for assistance in obtaining documentary proof that the stranger is a U.S. citizen. Planning to start a trip to a neighboring country the next day and with no time to get a U.S. passport, the stranger was told by a travel agent that any Notary could provide the proof of U.S. citizenship that foreign authorities will need to see. The stranger asks the Notary to supply whatever is needed.

The Ethical Imperative: The Notary directs the stranger to telephone a consulate of the neighboring nation for definitive information on the paperwork needed to visit that nation.

VI-B-2: Preparing Document Improper

The Notary who is not an attorney, or a professional duly trained or certified in a pertinent field, shall not prepare a document for another person or provide advice on how to fill out, draft or complete a document.

Illustration: The Notary is asked by a stranger to provide a "notarized affidavit of citizenship" that will allow the stranger to visit a neighboring country. An airline had informed the stranger that any Notary may prepare such a document.

The Ethical Imperative: The Notary informs the stranger that a nonattorney is not authorized to prepare documents for other persons. The Notary asks the stranger to compose the document after finding out what it must contain. Once the document is in its final form, the Notary will be able to witness the stranger's signature, administer an oath and execute a jurat certificate, as required for any affidavit.

Article C: Providing Unauthorized Advice

VI-C-1: Legal Counseling Improper

The Notary who is not an attorney, or a professional duly trained or certified in a pertinent field, shall not provide advice on how to act or proceed in a given legal matter that may or may not involve a notarial act.

Illustration: The Notary is asked by a friend, "Do you know anything about wills?" The friend then expresses a desire to make sure that a relative will receive all the friend's property in the event of death. The friend asks, "Can I just write out what I want and then have you notarize it?"

The Ethical Imperative: As a nonattorney, the Notary declines to offer legal advice about the preparation of a last will and testament, urging the friend to seek the advice of an attorney.

Article D: Providing Unauthorized Services

VI-D-1: Certifying Vital Record or Recordable Document Improper

The Notary shall not certify the accuracy and completeness of a copy if the original is a photocopy, a vital record or a recordable document, nor certify any hand-rendered reproduction.

Illustration: The Notary is asked by a stranger "to certify a copy of my birth certificate." The stranger needs a birth certificate for foreign travel but does not want to risk losing the "original."

The Ethical Imperative: The Notary declines to certify a copy of a birth certificate, because it is a vital record that only a custodian of vital statistics may properly certify; a Notary's "certification" of a birth, death or other vital record may lend credence to a counterfeit or tampered document.

Very likely, the "original" presented by the stranger is itself a certified copy and, for a modest fee, the stranger may obtain another such copy from the bureau of vital statistics in the locality of birth.

VI-D-2: Certifying Photograph Improper

The Notary shall not certify the accuracy or authenticity of a photograph.

Illustration: The Notary is asked by a stranger to notarize that person's signature on a document bearing text, jurat language and a photograph of the stranger at the end. The stranger directs the Notary to affix the seal partially over the photograph.

The Professional Choice: The Notary complies with the stranger's instruction. In notarizing a document with text, a signature and some form of jurat or acknowledgment certificate, the Notary may affix the seal partially over an attached photograph. The document's text may declare the accuracy or authenticity of the photograph, but the Notary's certificate may not.

VI-D-3: Certifying Translation Improper

The Notary shall not certify the accuracy or completeness of a translation.

Illustration: The Notary is asked by a stranger to "certify" a translation of that person's foreign birth certificate for an immigration petition.

The Ethical Imperative: The Notary declines to perform such a certification, because Notaries in the United States are not authorized to certify the accuracy of translations, though they may notarize the signature of a translator on a translator's declaration.

GUIDING PRINCIPLE VII

The Notary shall affix a seal on every notarized document and not allow this universally recognized symbol of office to be used by another or in an endorsement or promotion.

Standards of Professional and Ethical Practice

Article A: Affixation of Seal

VII-A-1: Seal Important on Every Document

The Notary shall affix a legible imprint or impression of an official seal on every document notarized.

Illustration: The Notary resides in a state that does not require Notaries to affix seals of office on notarized documents; however, using a seal is not prohibited and many Notaries do opt to affix a seal. The Notary ponders whether use of a seal justifies the expense.

The Professional Choice: Even though state law does not require a seal, the Notary opts to obtain and use one, believing it imparts a sense of ceremony and official completion to the act of notarizing that most document signers seem to expect and appreciate. The Notary also knows that a well-placed seal impression can deter forgers and eliminate potential recording problems when a document is sent out of state to a jurisdiction where Notaries use seals. The Notary decides that the minor expense of purchasing a seal is far outweighed by its advantages.

VII-A-2: Manual Affixation of Seal Necessary

The Notary shall manually affix every impression of the official seal, unless electronic affixation is expressly Permitted by law, in which case the Notary shall maintain exclusive control over the means of such affixation.

Illustration: The Notary considers whether it might be handy to "scan" the inked impression of the Notary seal and store it in a computer. That way, each notarial certificate may be printed out with a Notary seal already neatly and legibly affixed. Law in the Notary's state is silent about electronic affixation of seals.

The Professional Choice: Since state law does not expressly authorize electronic affixation of Notary seals, the Notary continues to affix the seal manually at the time of each notarization, keeping it under lock and key when not in use. The Notary realizes that putting an image of an official seal in a computer compounds the seal security problem. Persons with access to the computer would be able to print out the seal on unauthorized documents, or copy it for use on other computers.

VII-A-3: Preprinted Seal Disallowed

The Notary shall not affix nor allow the official seal to be affixed or preprinted on any certificate or document prior to the time of notarization.

Illustration: The Notary is asked by a supervisor for an impression of the Notary's seal so that it may be reprinted on multiple copies of certain standard office forms. "That way, we don't have to worry about smeared or illegible seal impressions," the supervisor says. The Notary is told that the resulting copies will be under the Notary's strict control.

The Ethical Imperative: The Notary refuses to allow the official seal to be preprinted on any document, because it would effectively mean surrendering control of the seal.

Article B: Control of Seal

VII-B-1: Safeguarding When Not in Use

The Notary shall safeguard the official seal to prevent its misuse by others when it is out of the Notary's sight.

Illustration: The Notary maintains a desk in a large and busy office with nearly 30 other desks nearby. The Notary finds it convenient to keep the official seal and journal at this desk.

The Professional Choice: The Notary always keeps the seal and journal in a locked drawer when not in use. The key is safeguarded on the Notary's person.

VII-B-2: Use or Possession by Another Improper

The Notary shall not allow the official seal to be used or possessed by another person.

Illustration: The Notary is asked by a coworker for permission to "borrow" the Notary's seal and sign the Notary's name until the coworker's commission is renewed. Having failed to keep track of the commission expiration date, the coworker tearfully claims that not being able to notarize may result in dismissal from the job.

The Ethical Imperative: Understanding that Notaries are commissioned to deter fraud and not to abet it, the Notary refuses to let another person use the official seal and title to perform deceptive notarizations that will amount to criminal acts on the part of both individuals. To help out, the Notary offers to notarize for any person referred by the coworker.

VII-B-3: Reproduction in Advertisement Improper

The Notary shall not allow others to use or reproduce the Notary's seal in a commercial advertisement, solicitation or testimonial.

Illustration: The Notary is asked by a stranger to notarize an affidavit. After signing the document in the Notary's presence, the stranger instructs the Notary to "be extra neat" and take special care in affixing the seal because "we intend to duplicate the affidavit by the thousands in advertisements" for a new product.

The Ethical Imperative: The Notary declines to notarize, not wanting the official signature, seal, certificate and title "Notary" reproduced in a commercial solicitation that may mislead some people into believing that the product is governmentally sanctioned or approved. A Notary need not investigate every transaction to ensure that a particular notarial certificate will not be reproduced, but the Notary should decline to notarize when having knowledge that the Notary's name or the words "Notary" or "notarized" will appear in a promotion.

Article C: Disposal of Seal

VII-C-1: Surrendering Seal to Employer Improper

The Notary shall not surrender the seal to an employer or supervisor upon termination of employment, even if the employer paid for the seal.

Illustration: The Notary gives an employer two weeks' notice before leaving for a new job. The employer responds that the Notary must surrender the seal before departing, since the employer paid for it.

The Ethical Imperative: The Notary informs the supervisor that the seal will not be surrendered, since it is the personalized symbol and certifying tool of the notarial office and its use by anyone but the Notary would be unlawful.

VII-C-2: Destruction or Defacement Necessary

To prevent its misuse by others, the Notary shall destroy or deface the official seal when the term of office it denotes ends or is cut short by revocation or resignation, provided the law does not prescribe another disposition.

Illustration: The Notary moves to another state for a new job.

The Professional Choice: Before moving, the Notary sends a letter of resignation to the state Notary-regulating office by certified mail, indicating a date of resignation. On that date, the Notary defaces the seal so that it may not be misused.

GUIDING PRINCIPLE VIII

The Notary shall record every notarial act in a bound journal or other secure recording device, and safeguard it as an important public record.

Standards of Professional and Ethical Practice

Article A: Record of Notarial Acts

VIII-A-1: Entering Every Official Act Critical

The Notary shall maintain a complete, sequential record of every notarial act performed by the Notary in a bound journal or other secure recording device allowed by law.

Illustration: The Notary resides in a state where keeping a record of notarial acts is not required by law. The Notary ponders whether to document each notarization in a recordbook.

The Professional Choice: Even though state law does not mandate record keeping, the Notary opts to maintain a journal in the belief that all responsible and businesslike public servants should keep a record of their official activities. In addition, the journal will prove invaluable as protective evidence of the Notary's use of reasonable care in the event of a lawsuit.

VIII-A-2: Essential Components of Entry

For every notarial act performed, the corresponding entry in the Notary's journal shall contain, at least: the date, time and type of the notarial act; the date and description of the document or transaction; the name, address and signature of each person whose signature was notarized or who served as a witness; a description of the evidence used to identify any signer who is not personally known; and the fee charged for the notarial act.

Illustration: The Notary is asked by a stranger to notarize "some sensitive personal papers." The stranger presents only the signature pages of the documents. "They relate to a very messy and painful divorce," the stranger tells the Notary, "and there's no need for anyone but myself, my ex-spouse and our lawyers to know the details." The stranger keeps the text of all the documents hidden from the Notary.

The Professional Choice: The Notary refuses to notarize unless handed all pages of each document. "I have no intention of reading or divulging information from your documents," the Notary tells the stranger, "but I do have a need to scan them for certain data to record in my journal, including each document's title and number of pages." The Notary further explains that the act of notarization that will protect the stranger's rights in the divorce necessarily requires surrendering to the public record certain minimally descriptive information about the transaction; it is part of the small cost of protection assured by the notarial act.

VIII-A-3: Entry Contemporaneous with Act

A complete record of any notarial act performed by the Notary shall be entered in the journal at the actual time of the notarial act, not before and not after.

Illustration: The Notary arrives at the home of a client to notarize documents but forgot to bring the journal of notarial acts along. The client urges the Notary to proceed with the notarization anyway, and promises to stop by the Notary's office later to sign the journal.

The Professional Choice: Declining to notarize without the journal, the Notary leaves to retrieve it and returns shortly to the client's home. The Notary realizes the importance of securing a journal signature and ID description at the time of the notarization rather than later, when a change of mind by the signer might cause the notarization to be falsely challenged.

Article B: Public Inspection

VIII-B-1: Limiting Access to Journal

The Notary shall show or provide a copy of any entry in the journal of notarial acts to any person identified by the Notary who presents a written and signed request specifying the month and year, the document type, and the name of the signer(s) for the respective notarization.

Illustration: The Notary is approached by a stranger who claims to be an attorney representing a person for whom the Notary had notarized a document several months earlier. The stranger says the document is now at issue in a lawsuit, and asks to look at the journal of notarial acts.

The Professional Choice: As a public official and servant, the Notary understands that private citizens may have a legitimate need to verify facts related to a particular notarization by looking at the journal. The Notary asks the stranger to present identification, as well as a written, signed request stating the month and year of the notarization, the name of the person whose signature was notarized, and the type of document. The Notary explains that the stranger may only see the entries specified in writing, to respect the privacy of other signers and discourage opportunistic "fishing expeditions."

VIII-B-2: Control of Record Essential

To prevent loss, theft or tampering, the Notary shall safeguard and maintain control over the journal of notarial acts, and not surrender it to any person who does not present a subpoena or other lawful written authorization.

Illustration: The Notary is asked by an acquaintance to see a particular entry in the journal of notarial acts, through presentation of a written, signed request. After viewing the entry, the acquaintance asks to make a photocopy. When the Notary responds that there is no photocopier available on the premises, the acquaintance asks, "May I take the journal to the copy shop around the corner and come right back?"

The Professional Choice: The Notary declines, explaining, "It's my policy never to surrender control of the journal of notarial acts except when presented with a subpoena." As a courtesy, the Notary offers to make a copy of the journal entry that evening, if the acquaintance will return the next day.

Article C: Disposal of Journal

VIII-C-1: Surrender to Employer Improper

The Notary shall not surrender the journal to an employer upon termination of employment, even if the employer paid for the journal, unless law expressly authorizes.

Illustration: The Notary gives notice of intent to leave for a new job in two weeks. The Notary's supervisor says that the firm will require the official journal of notarial acts to be left behind, since "it contains important information for our business records."

The Professional Choice: The Notary refuses to surrender the journal to the employer. The journal is the official record of a particular notarial officer; it must be kept in the custody of that officer, who will be solely accountable for its accuracy and its availability as evidence for the public benefit. However, the Notary is not prohibited from providing the firm with copies of all entries made in connection with its business.

VIII-C-2: Storage of Record

In the absence of official rules for disposal of the journal of notarial acts, the former Notary shall store and safeguard each journal at least 10 years from the date of the last entry in the journal.

Illustration: The Notary reports for work at a new job to find that there are a more than sufficient number of Notaries on staff to handle the office's business. With the commission about to expire, the Notary decides not to renew and to "retire" as a Notary.

The Professional Choice: On the day after commission expiration, the Notary stores the journal of notarial acts in the locked fireproof cabinet used to store all of the Notary's important personal documents. The Notary attaches a note on the cover that the journal must not be discarded or destroyed prior to a particular date, 10 years from the last entry in the journal. Notaries in states where statutory limits on civil lawsuits extend beyond 10 years may opt to preserve the journal as potential evidence as long as they feel it prudent.

GUIDING PRINCIPLE IX

The Notary shall respect the privacy of each signer and not divulge or use personal or proprietary information disclosed during execution of a notarial act for other than an official purpose.

Standards of Professional and Ethical Practice

Article A: Needless Intrusions

IX-A-1: Scrutinizing of Text

The Notary shall scrutinize the non-notarial text of a document for two purposes only: to ascertain if it appears complete and to extract data for recording in the journal of notarial acts.

Illustration: The Notary is asked by a man and woman to notarize their prenuptial agreement. After they identify themselves and hand over the document, the couple is distracted for several minutes in making a telephone call. Alone with the document, the Notary is tempted to closely read its provisions.

The Ethical Imperative: The Notary intrudes no further than to scan the document for blank spaces and missing pages, and to glean certain bits of data to record in the journal, including the document's title, date and number of pages. The Notary realizes that reading the document would be an invasion of the couple's privacy and a breach of public trust.

IX-A-2: Extracting or Copying Unnecessary Information

The Notary shall not needlessly extract or copy information from the text of a notarized document or from other documents possessed by its signer.

Illustration: The Notary observes that a coworker Notary always makes and keeps a copy of each document notarized and of each ID card presented. The coworker explains, "It's protection for me in case I'm sued."

The Professional Choice: The Notary points out to the coworker that this policy constitutes an unwarranted invasion of each signer's privacy, and risks the possibility of theft or loss of a copy and unauthorized dissemination of sensitive personal information. The Notary explains that a detailed journal entry for each notarial act that includes a description of any ID card presented and a signature will serve the same protective purpose in the event of a lawsuit.

Article B: Unauthorized Use of Information

IX-B-1: Revealing Document Particulars Improper

The Notary shall not divulge information about the circumstances of a notarial act to any person who does not have clear lawful authority and a need to know.

Illustration: The Notary is notarizing mortgage papers for a stranger when a close friend walks in. After the signer has left, the friend asks, "That person just bought the house down the street from me. Did you happen to notice the selling price?"

The Ethical Imperative: Though by chance noting the price on one of the documents just notarized, the Notary declines to inform the friend about any particulars in the documents. The Notary would regard such a revelation as an invasion of the stranger's privacy and a breach of public trust.

IX-B-2: Personal Use of Information Improper

The Notary shall not use for personal gain any information extracted from the text of a document that he or she has notarized.

Illustration: Notarizing a heavy volume of documents for walk-in customers every day, the Notary is approached by the agent of a company that prepares and files homestead documents for homeowners. The agent offers to pay the Notary a finder's fee for providing the names and addresses of new home purchasers from the many deeds notarized daily.

The Ethical Imperative: The Notary declines the offer, refusing to profit personally from use of information extracted from the text of notarized documents.

IX-B-3: Random Journal Perusal Improper

Except for the access allowed by Standard VIII-B-1, the Notary shall not allow perusal of the journal of notarial acts by any person who does not present a subpoena or other evidence of official authorization.

Illustration: The Notary is approached by a stranger who presents identification and a written request to see a particular entry in the Notary's journal pertaining to the notarization of a deceased spouse's signature on a deed. The signed request is specific about the date of notarization and the type of document. The Notary finds the requested journal entry, but, before showing it, covers other entries on the same page. After studying the information, the stranger asks to look at other entries in the journal, fearing that the deceased spouse "may have been involved in other scams to cheat me out of property."

The Ethical Imperative: The Notary declines to show the stranger any other journal entries unless the person is equally specific about these recorded notarial acts. The Notary is sensitive about all signers' privacy and will not reveal their transactions to anyone who cannot be specific or present a subpoena or other evidence of official authorization.

GUIDING PRINCIPLE X

The Notary shall seek instruction on notarization, and keep current on the laws, practices and requirements of the notarial office.

Standards of Professional and Ethical Practice

Article A: Seeking Knowledge

X-A-1: Studying Official Literature Essential

The Notary shall study all official pamphlets, handbooks, manuals and other literature pertaining to the performance of notarial acts in the Notary's jurisdiction.

Illustration: An employee is asked by a supervisor to become a Notary. The supervisor provides a telephone number to call to request commission application materials. The employee soon receives an application form, an instruction sheet and a slim brochure titled "Notary Handbook."

The Professional Choice: The would-be Notary completes and returns the application form. While waiting for the new commission, the employee studies the "Notary Handbook."

X-A-2: Studying Laws and Regulations Essential

The Notary shall study all laws, regulations and official directives that pertain to the performance of notarial acts in the Notary's jurisdiction.

Illustration: After receiving a commission in the mail, the first-time Notary follows instructions to file an oath of office and purchases a seal. However, the Notary still feels inadequately prepared to perform official acts, since the "Notary Handbook" offers just a minimal description of notarial duties, with no specific instructions or practical guidelines.

The Professional Choice: The new Notary obtains copies of the statute sections cited in the "Handbook." The Notary carefully studies these laws and keeps them handy at work.

X-A-3: Supplemental Guidance Often Necessary

In order to achieve a solid understanding of the basic principles and practices of notarization, the Notary shall be proactive in seeking out expert guidance and in supplementing any official training or materials with those provided by respected educational institutions and professional organizations.

Illustration: The newly commissioned Notary has studied the state's Notary laws and "Notary Handbook," but finds they offer no practical procedures and guidelines for performing notarial duties. The Notary still lacks confidence about how to notarize.

The Professional Choice: The new Notary finds a helpful, experienced Notary, who tells the beginner to call if any questions arise while performing a notarization. The experienced Notary also lends the new Notary several publications from professional organizations for Notaries.

X-A-4: Continuing Education Essential

The Notary shall keep current on new laws and regulations and on any other developments that affect the performance of notarial acts in the Notary's jurisdiction.

Illustration: The Notary is asked to notarize a document by a stranger who presents a "green card" as proof of identity. When the Notary explains that such a card is not on the statutory list of acceptable IDs, the stranger claims to have no other IDs. However, another Notary advises that a recent change to the state's Notary code now allows use of green cards to identify signers, and shows an announcement of the law change in a periodical from a professional organization for Notaries.

The Professional Choice: The Notary completes the notarization, resolving to subscribe to the publication in order to keep abreast of new laws affecting notarial duties.

Article B: Dispensing Knowledge

X-B-1: Providing Expertise to Others

The Notary shall freely provide notarial expertise to less experienced Notaries and step forward to offer needed corrective advice on the proper performance of notarial acts.

Illustration: The Notary observes that another Notary in the same office consistently fails to ask document signers to present identification.

The Ethical Imperative: The Notary approaches the coworker and tactfully explains the disservice to the public and the potential personal liability of failing to identify strangers.

Article C: Maintaining Standards

X-C-1: Reporting Misconduct

The Notary shall report to the commissioning authority violations of the statutes, regulations and directives governing the conduct of Notaries.

Illustration: The Notary observes that another Notary in the same office consistently fails to ask document signers to present identification. After the coworker ignores repeated tactful warnings about the danger of this policy, the Notary reports the misconduct to their supervisor. However, even after a word from the supervisor, the colleague remains cavalier and careless about notarial duties. "I don't care," the coworker tells the Notary, "If they fire me, they fire me."

The Ethical Imperative: Worried that the coworker's carelessness will be exploited to facilitate frauds, the Notary sends a letter to the state Notary-commissioning authority, detailing the colleague's habitual misconduct. ■

Notary Public Regulators

To obtain a Notary Public commission application or other forms, or to ask questions about operating as a Notary in your state, contact the National Notary Association or your state Notary Public Regulator using the contact information provided on the following pages.

In addition, there are many useful resources available at state and territorial official websites or at the NNA website, www.NationalNotary.org. The NNA is headquartered at 9350 De Soto Avenue, Chatsworth, CA 91311-4926 — telephone (818) 739-4000.

Alabama
Office of Secretary of State
Admin. Services, Notaries Public
State Capitol, Rm. S-105
P.O. Box 5616
Montgomery, AL 36103-5616
1-334-242-7205

Alaska
Office of Lieutenant Governor
Notary Public Office
240 Main St., Suite 301
Juneau, AK 99801
1-907-465-3509

American Samoa
American Samoa Government
Office of Governor
Secretary of American Samoa
A.P. Lutali Executive Office Bldg., Utulei
Pago Pago, American Samoa 96799
1-684-633-4116

Arizona
Office of Secretary of State
Business Services Division
Notary Section
1700 West Washington, 7th Floor
Phoenix, AZ 85007-2888
1-602-542-4758

Arkansas
Office of Secretary of State
Business & Commercial Services Div.
1401 W. Capitol Ave., Ste. 250
Little Rock, AR 72201-1094
1-501-682-3409

California
Office of Secretary of State
Notary Public Section
P.O. Box 942877
Sacramento, CA 94277-0001
1-916-653-3595

Colorado
Office of Secretary of State
Bus. and Licensing Div.
Notary Program, Ext. 9500
1700 Broadway, Suite 200
Denver, CO 80290
1-303-894-2200

Connecticut
Office of Secretary of the State
Notary Public Unit
P.O. Box 150470
Hartford, CT 06115-0470
1-860-509-6100

Delaware
Office of Secretary of State
Notary Public Section
401 Federal St., Suite 4
Dover, DE 19901
1-302-739-4111

District of Columbia
Office of Secretary of District
Office of Notary Commissions & Authentications
441 4th St. NW, Ste. 810 S.
Washington, DC 20001-2700
1-202-727-3117

Florida
Department of State
Division of Corporations
Notary Commissions & Certifications
P.O. Box 6327
Tallahassee, FL 32314
1-850-245-6975

Georgia
Georgia Superior Court Clerks' Cooperative Authority
Notary Division
1875 Century Blvd., Suite 100
Atlanta, GA 30345
1-404-327-6023

Guam
Office of Attorney General
Administration Division
287 West O'Brien Drive
Hagatna, GU 96910
1-671-475-3324

Hawaii
Department of Attorney General
Notary Public Program
425 Queen St.
Honolulu, HI 96813
1-808-586-1216

Idaho
Office of Secretary of State
Notary Public Department
450 N. 4th Street
Boise, ID 83720-3720
1-208-332-2810

Illinois
Office of Secretary of State
Department of Index
111 East Monroe St.
Springfield, IL 62756
1-217-782-7017

Indiana
Office of Secretary of State
Notary Department
State House, Room 201
200 W. Washington St.
Indianapolis, IN 46204
1-317-232-6542

Iowa
Office of Secretary of State
Notary Division
Lucas Building, 1st Floor
321 East 12th Street
Des Moines, IA 50319
1-515-281-5204

Kansas
Office of Secretary of State
Notary Clerk
Memorial Hall, 1st Floor
120 S.W. 10th Ave.
Topeka, KS 66612-1594
1-785-296-2239

Kentucky
Office of Secretary of State
Notary Branch
P.O. Box 821
700 Capital Ave., Suite 86
Frankfort, KY 40601
1-502-564-3490

Louisiana
Office of Secretary of State
Notary Division
P.O. Box 94125
Baton Rouge, LA 70804-9125
1-225-922-0507

Maine
Department of Secretary of State
Bur. of Corporations, Elections, and Commissions
Corps., UCC & Commissions Div.
Notary Public Section
101 State House Station
(111 Sewall St. 4th Floor)
Augusta, ME 04333-0101
1-207-624-7752

Maryland
Office of Secretary of State
Notary Division
16 Francis Street
Annapolis MD 21401
1-410-974-5521

Massachusetts
Office of Secretary of Commonwealth
Public Records Division
Commissions Section
One Ashburton Place, Room 1719
Boston, MA 02108
1-617-727-2832

Michigan
Office of Secretary of State
Office of Great Seal
7064 Crowner Dr.
Lansing, MI 48918
1-888-767-6424

Minnesota
Office of Secretary of State
60 Empire Drive, Suite 100
St. Paul, MN 55103
1-651-296-2803

Mississippi
Office of Secretary of State
Business Services Division
Notary Section
700 North Street
Jackson, MS 39215-1020
1-601-359-1615

Missouri
Office of Secretary of State
Commissions Division
P.O. Box 784
Jefferson City, MO 65102
1-573-751-2783

Montana
Office of Secretary of State
Notary & Certification Services
P.O. Box 202801
Helena, MT 59620-2801
1-406-444-5379

Nebraska
Office of Secretary of State
Business Services Division
Notary Public Section
State Capitol, Room 1301
Lincoln, NE 68509-5104
1-402-471-2558

Nevada
Office of Secretary of State
Notary Division
101 N. Carson St., Suite 3
Carson City, NV 89701
1-775-684-5708

New Hampshire
Office of Secretary of State
State House, Room 204
107 North Main St.
Concord, NH 03301
1-603-271-3242

New Jersey
Department of Treasury
Division of Revenue
Bus. Support Services Bur.
Notary Public Unit, P.O. Box 452
Trenton, NJ 08646-0452
1-609-633-8258

New Mexico
Office of Secretary of State
Bus. Services, Notary Division
State Capitol North Annex
325 Don Gaspar, Suite 300
Santa Fe, NM 87503
1-505-827-3600

New York
Department of State
Division of Licensing Services
P.O. Box 22001
Albany, NY 12201-2001
1-518-474-4429

North Carolina
Office of Secretary of State
Notary Public Section
P.O. Box 29626
Raleigh, NC 27626-0626
1-919-807-2219

North Dakota
Office of Secretary of State
Administrative/Licensing Division
600 E. Boulevard Avenue, Dept. 108
Bismarck, ND 58505-0500
1-707-328-2901

Northern Marianas
Commonwealth of Northern
Mariana Islands
Office of Attorney General
Administration Bldg., Box 10007
Capital Hill
Saipan, MP 96950
1-670-664-2341

Ohio
Ohio Secretary of State
Notary Commissions Clerk
180 E. Broad Street, Room 103
Columbus, OH 43215
1-614-644-4559

Oklahoma
Office of Secretary of State
Notary Public Services
2300 North Lincoln, Room 101
Oklahoma City, OK 73105
1-405-521-2516

Oregon
Office of Secretary of State
Corporation Division
255 Capitol St. N.E., Suite 151
Salem, OR 97310-1327
1-503-986-2200

Pennsylvania
Department of State
Division of Legislation and Notaries
North Office Building, Room 210
Harrisburg, PA 17120-0029
1-717-787-5280

Puerto Rico
Supreme Court of Puerto Rico
Office of Notarial Inspection
Judicial Center (3rd Floor)
Muñoz Rivera Ave.
P.O. Box 190860
San Juan, PR 00919-0860
1-787-763-8816

Rhode Island
Office of Secretary of State
Division of Business Services
Notary Public Section
148 West River St.
Providence, RI 02904-2615
1-401-222-3040

South Carolina
Office of Secretary of State
Notary Public Division
1205 Pendleton St. Suite 525
Columbia, SC 29201
1-803-734-2512

South Dakota
Office of Secretary of State
Notary Administrator
500 E. Capitol Ave., Suite 204
Pierre, SD 57501
1-605-773-3537

Tennessee
Department of State
Division of Business Services
Notary Commissions Services
312 Rosa L. Parks Ave., 6th floor
Nashville, TN 37243
1-615-741-3699

Texas
Office of Secretary of State
Statutory Documents Section
Notary Public Unit
P.O. Box 13375
Austin, TX 78711-3375
1-512-463-5705

Utah
Office of Lieutenant Governor
Notary Office
Utah State Capitol Complex, Ste. 220
Salt Lake City, UT 84114
1-801-538-1041

Vermont
Office of Secretary of State
Vermont State Archives & Records Admin.
Montpelier, VT 05633-7701
1-802-828-3287

Virginia
Office of Secretary of Commonwealth
Notary Public Division
P.O. Box 1795
Richmond, VA 23218-1795
1-804-786-2441

Virgin Islands, U.S.
Office of Lieutenant Governor
18 Kongens Gade
Charlotte Amalie
St. Thomas, VI 00802
1-340-774-2991

Washington
Department of Licensing
Business & Professional Licenses
Notaries Public Unit
P.O. Box 9027
Olympia, WA 98507-9027
1-360-664-1531

West Virginia
Office of Secretary of State
Bus. & Licensing Division
Notary Administrator
Capitol Building 1, Suite 157-K
1900 Kanawha Blvd., East
Charleston, WV 25305-0770
1-304-558-6000

Wisconsin
Department of Financial Institutions
Notary Public & Trademarks
345 West Washington, 3rd Floor
Madison, WI 53703
1-608-266-8915

Wyoming
Office of Secretary of State
Notary Division
State Capitol Building
200 W. 24th
Cheyenne, WY 82002-0020
1-307-777-5335

Bureaus of Vital Statistics

Notaries Public are not permitted to make certified copies of any vital records. Persons requesting notarization or certified copies of birth or death certificates should be referred to the respective state public office (below) that can provide certified copies of vital records. Persons requiring copies of foreign records should contact the appropriate consulate in the United States.

Alabama
Vital Records
Department of Public Health
P.O. Box 5625
Montgomery, AL 36103-5625

Alaska
Bureau of Vital Statistics
Department of Health &
Social Services
5441 Commercial Blvd.
P.O. Box 110675
Juneau, AK 99801

Arizona
Office of Vital Records
Department of Health Services
P.O. Box 3887
Phoenix, AZ 85030-3887

Arkansas
Division of Vital Records
Department of Health
4815 West Markham Street, Slot 44
Little Rock, AR 72205-3867

California
Office of Vital Records
Department of Health Services
P.O. Box 997410, MS: 5103
Sacramento, CA 95899-7410

Colorado
Vital Records Section
Department of Health
4300 Cherry Creek Drive South
Denver, CO 80246-1530

Connecticut
Department of Public Health
State Office of Vital Records
410 Capitol Avenue, MS #11VRS
P.O. Box 340308
Hartford, CT 06134-0308

Delaware
Health Statistics Center
Office of Vital Statistics
Jesse S. Cooper Building
417 Federal Street
Dover, DE 19901

District of Columbia
Vital Records Division
899 North Capitol Street NE,
1st Floor
Washington, DC 20002

Florida
Office of Vital Statistics
1217 North Pearl Street
P.O. Box 210
Jacksonville, FL 32231

Georgia
Vital Records
2600 Skyland Drive
Atlanta, GA 30319-3640

Hawaii
State Department of Health
Office of Health Status Monitoring
Issuance/Vital Statistics Section
P.O. Box 3378
Honolulu, HI 96801

Idaho
Vital Statistics Unit
450 West State Street, 1st Floor
P.O. Box 83720
Boise, ID 83720-0036

Illinois
Division of Vital Records
Department of Public Health
605 West Jefferson Street
Springfield, IL 62702-5097

Indiana
Vital Records Department
State Department of Health
2 North Meridian Street
Indianapolis, IN 46204

Iowa
Department of Public Health
Bureau of Vital Records
Lucas Office Building, 1st Floor
321 East 12th Street
Des Moines, IA 50319-0075

Kansas
Office of Vital Statistics
1000 SW Jackson Street, Suite 120
Topeka, KS 66612-2221

Kentucky
Office of Vital Statistics
Department for Health Services
275 East Main Street, 1E-A
Frankfort, KY 40621-0001

Louisiana
Vital Records Registry
P.O. Box 60630
New Orleans, LA 70160

Maine
Vital Statistics
220 Capitol Street
11 State House Station
Augusta, ME 04333-0011

Maryland
Division of Vital Records
Department of Health
6550 Reisterstown Road
Baltimore, MD 21215

Massachusetts
Registry of Vital Records and
Statistics
150 Mount Vernon Street, 1st Floor
Dorchester, MA 02125-3105

Michigan
Vital Records Request
P.O. Box 30721
Lansing, MI 48909

Minnesota
Minnesota Department of Health
Central Cashiering — Vital Records
P.O. Box 64499
St. Paul, MN 55164-0499

Mississippi
Mississippi Vital Records
P.O. Box 1700
Jackson, MS 39215-1700

Missouri
Department of Health
Bureau of Vital Records
930 Wildwood
P.O. Box 570
Jefferson City, MO 65102-0570

Montana
Office of Vital Statistics
P.O. Box 4210
111 North Sanders, Room 6
Helena, MT 59604

Nebraska
Vital Statistics
Department of Health
1033 "O" Street, Suite 130
P.O. Box 95065
Lincoln, NE 68509-5065

Nevada
Office of Vital Records
4150 Technology Way, Suite 104
Carson City, NV 89706

New Hampshire
Department of State
Division of Vital Records
Administration
71 South Fruit Street
Concord, NH 03301-2410

New Jersey
Vital Statistics
Customer Service
P.O. Box 370
Trenton, NJ 08625-0370

New Mexico
Vital Records and Health Statistics
1105 South St. Francis Drive
Santa Fe, NM 87502

New York
State Department of Health
Vital Records Certification Unit
P.O. Box 2602
Albany, NY 12220-2602

New York City
NYC Department of Health and
Mental Hygiene
Office of Vital Records
125 Worth Street, CN4, Room 133
New York, NY 10013

North Carolina
Vital Records
1903 Mail Service Center
Raleigh, NC 27699-1903

North Dakota
Division of Vital Records
600 East Boulevard Avenue,
Dept. 301
Bismarck, ND 58505-0200

Ohio
Department of Health
Vital Statistics
P.O. Box 15098
Columbus, OH 43215-0098

Oklahoma
Vital Records Service
State Department of Health
1000 Northeast 10th Street
Oklahoma City, OK 73117

Oregon
Vital Records
P.O. Box 14050
Portland, OR 97293-0050

Pennsylvania
Division of Vital Records
101 South Mercer Street, Room 401
P.O. Box 1528
New Castle, PA 16101

Rhode Island
Office of Vital Records
Department of Health
3 Capitol Hill Road, Room 101
Providence, RI 02908-5097

South Carolina
Office of Vital Records
South Carolina DHEC
2600 Bull Street
Columbia, SC 29201

South Dakota
Vital Records
207 East Missouri Avenue, Suite 1A
Pierre, SD 57501

Tennessee
Tennessee Vital Records
1st Floor, Central Services Building
421 5th Avenue North
Nashville, TN 37243

Texas
Texas Vital Records
Department of State Health Services
P.O. Box 12040
Austin, TX 78711-2040

Utah
Vital Records and Statistics
Cannon Health Building
288 North 1460 West
P.O. Box 141012
Salt Lake City, UT 84114-1012

Vermont
Department of Health
Vital Records Section
108 Cherry Street
P.O. Box 70
Burlington, VT 05402-0070

Virginia
Office of Vital Records
P.O. Box 1000
Richmond, VA 23218-1000

Washington
Department of Health
Center for Health Statistics
P.O. Box 9709
Olympia, WA 98507-9709

West Virginia
Vital Registration
350 Capitol Street, Room 165
Charleston, WV 25301-3701

Wisconsin
Vital Records
1 West Wilson Street
P.O. Box 309
Madison, WI 53701-0309

Wyoming
Vital Statistics Services
Hathaway Building
Cheyenne, WY 82002

American Samoa
Office of Records and Vital Statistics
LBJ Tropical Medical Center
Department of Health Services
American Samoa Government
Pago Pago, AS 96799

Guam
Office of Vital Statistics
Department of Public Health
123 Chalan Kareta
Mangilao, GU, 96913

Northern Mariana Islands
Bureau of Health Planning
Statistics Office
P.O. Box 500409 CK
Saipan, MP 96950-0409

Panama Canal Zone
Passport Vital Records Office
U.S. Department of State
1111 19th Street NW, Suite 510
Washington, DC 20036

Puerto Rico
Department of Health
Demographic Registry
P.O. Box 11854
Fernández Juncos Station
San Juan, PR 00910

Virgin Islands (St. Croix)
Department of Health
Vital Statistics
Charles Harwood Memorial Hospital
St. Croix, VI 00820

Virgin Islands
(St. Thomas, St. John)
Department of Health
Registrar of Vital Statistics
Knud Hansen Complex
St. Thomas, VI 0080

Hague Convention Nations

The nations listed on the following pages are parties to a treaty called *The Hague Convention Abolishing the Requirement of Legalization for Foreign Public Documents.*

Treaty Simplifies Authentication. A Notary's signature on documents that are exchanged between these nations may be authenticated (verified as valid for the benefit of the recipient in the foreign nation) by your state's Notary regulating office attachment of a single certificate of authenticity called an *apostille.* The *apostille* (French for "notation") is the only authentication certificate necessary. Nations not subscribing to this Hague Convention may require as many as five or six separate authenticating certificates from different governmental agencies, domestic and foreign.

How to Request an *Apostille*. To obtain an *apostille*, contact your State's Notary regulating office.

It is not the Notary's responsibility to obtain an *apostille*; it is the responsibility of the party needing authentication

Hague Convention Nations. The nations listed below participate in the Hague Convention. Footnotes reflect information likely to be of interest to Notaries and the clients they serve in the United States and its territories. Please note that some nations listed may not recognize the participation of every other nation listed. To verify recognition between nations, consult the website of the Hague Conference on Private International Law at http://www.hcch.net/index_en.php.

Albania
Andorra[13]
Antigua and Barbuda[13]
Argentina[1]
Armenia[13]
Australia
Austria
Azerbaijan[13]
Bahamas[13]
Bahrain[13]
Barbados[13]
Belarus
Belgium[8]
Belize[13]
Bosnia and Herzegovina[2]
Botswana[13]
Brunei Darussalam[13]
Bulgaria
Cape Verde[13]
Colombia[13]
Cook Islands[13]
Costa Rica
Croatia[2]
Cyprus
Czech Republic
Denmark[3]
Dominica[13]
Dominican Republic[13]
Ecuador
El Salvador[13]
Estonia
Fiji[13]
Finland
France[4]
Georgia[5]
Germany[8]
Greece
Grenada[13]
Honduras[13]
Hong Kong[6]
Hungary
Iceland
India
Ireland
Israel
Italy
Japan
Kazakhstan[13]
Korea, Republic of
Kyrgyzstan[13,14]
Latvia
Lesotho[13]
Liberia[8,13]
Liechtenstein[13]
Lithuania
Luxembourg
Macao[6]
Macedonia[2]
Malawi[13]
Malta
Marshall Islands[13]
Mauritius[13]
Mexico
Moldova, Republic of[13,18]
Monaco
Mongolia[13,19]
Montenegro[2]
Namibia[13]
Netherlands[9]
New Zealand[7]
Nicaragua
Niue[13]
Norway
Oman[13]

---

1. Argentina does not recognize the extension of the Convention by the United Kingdom to the Malvinas (Falkland Islands), South Georgia, South Sandwich Islands and the Argentine Antarctic Sector (British Antarctic Territory). See n. 11.
2. The former Socialist Federal Republic of Yugoslavia was a party to the Convention. Only the successor states of Bosnia and Herzegovina, Croatia, the Republic of Macedonia, Montenegro, Serbia and Slovenia have confirmed that the Convention still applies.
3. The participation of Denmark does not extend to Greenland and the Faro Islands.
4. The participation of France is extended to the entire territory of the French Republic, including French Guyana, French Polynesia, Guadeloupe, Martinique, Mayotte, New Caledonia, Reunion, St. Barthelemy, St. Martin, St. Pierre and Miquelon, and Wallis and Futuna.
5. The participation of Georgia does not extend to Abkhazia and South Ossetia.
6. Hong Kong and Macao retained their status as Hague nations after control was returned to China on July 1, 1997 (Hong Kong) and December 20, 1999 (Macao).
7. The participation of New Zealand does not extend to Tokelau.
8. The Convention does not apply between Liberia and the United States, Belgium or Germany.
9. The participation of the Netherlands is extended to Aruba and the Netherlands Antilles.

Panama
Peru[16]
Poland
Portugal[10]
Romania
Russian Federation
Saint Kitts and Nevis[13]
Saint Lucia[13]
Saint Vincent and the Grenadines[13]
Samoa[13]
San Marino[13]
Sao Tome and Principe[13]
Serbia[2]
Seychelles[13]
Slovakia
Slovenia[2]
South Africa
Spain[17]
Suriname
Swaziland[13]
Sweden
Switzerland
Tonga[13]
Trinidad and Tobago[13]
Turkey
Ukraine
United Kingdom[1,11]
United States[8,12]
Uruguay
Uzbekistan[13,15]
Vanuatu[13]
Venezuela

Inquiries. Persons having questions about *The Hague Convention Abolishing the Requirement of Legalization for Foreign Public Documents* may address their inquiries to:

U.S. Dept. of State
Authentications Office
518 23rd Street N.W.
State Annex 1
Washington, DC 20520
(202) 647-5002

10. The participation of Portugal is extended to the entire territory of the Republic of Portugal, including the Azores and Madeira.

11. The participation of the United Kingdom of Great Britain and Northern Ireland is extended to Anguilla, Bermuda, British Antarctic Territory, British Virgin Islands, Cayman Islands, Falkland Islands, Gibraltar, Guernsey, Isle of Man, Jersey, Montserrat, St. Helena and Turks and Caicos Islands.

12. The United States includes American Samoa, District of Columbia, Guam, Northern Mariana Islands, Puerto Rico and U.S. Virgin Islands.

13. This nation is not a member of the Hague Conference on Private International Law but is a party to *The Hague Convention Abolishing the Requirement of Legalization for Foreign Public Documents*.

14. The Convention will not enter into force between Kyrgyzstan and Austria, Belgium, Germany, or Greece.

15. The Convention will not enter into force between Uzbekistan and Austria, Belgium, Germany, or Greece.

16. The Convention will not enter into force between Peru and Germany or Greece.

17. The Ministry of Justice of Spain has put in place a new system for the issuance of *Apostilles*, which includes the possibility to issue both electronic and paper *Apostilles* (Note dated 23 June 2011).

18. The Convention will not enter into force between Moldova and Germany.

19. The Convention will not enter into force between Mongolia and Austria, Belgium, Finland, Germany, or Greece.

About the NNA

Since 1957, the National Notary Association — a nonprofit educational organization — has served the nation's Notaries Public with a wide variety of instructional programs and services.

As the country's clearinghouse for information on Notary laws, customs and practices, the NNA educates Notaries through publications, seminars, webinars, online training, annual conferences, its website and the NNA Hotline that offers immediate answers to specific questions about notarization.

The Association is perhaps most widely known as the preeminent source of information for and about Notaries. NNA works include the following:

- *The National Notary*, a magazine for NNA members featuring how-to articles and practical tips on notarizing

- *Notary Bulletin*, an online newsletter that keeps NNA members and customers up to date on developments affecting Notaries, especially new state laws and regulations

- *Sorry, No Can Do!* series, four volumes that help Notaries explain to customers and bosses why some requests for notarizations are improper and cannot be accommodated

- *U.S. Notary Reference Manual*, an invaluable resource for any person relying upon the authenticity and correctness of legal documents

- *Notary Public Practices & Glossary*, a definitive reference book on notarial procedures and widely hailed as the Notary's bible

- State *Notary Law Primers*, short guidebooks that explain a state's Notary statutes in easy-to-understand language

- *The Notary Public Code of Professional Responsibility*, a comprehensive and detailed code of ethical and professional conduct for Notaries

- *The Model Notary Act*, prototype legislation conceived in 1973 and updated in 1984, 2002 and 2010 by an NNA-recruited panel of secretaries of state, legislators and attorneys, and regularly used by state legislatures in revising their Notary laws

- *Notary Signing Agent Training Course*, a manual covering every aspect of signing agent procedures that prepares candidates for the Notary Signing Agent Certification Examination developed by the NNA

- Public-service pamphlets informing the general public about the function of a Notary, including *What Is A Notary Public?* printed in English and Spanish

In addition, the NNA offers the highest quality professional supplies, including official seals and stamps, embossers, recordkeeping journals, jurat stamps, thumbprinting devices and notarial certificates.

Though dedicated primarily to educating and assisting Notaries, the NNA supports implementing effective Notary laws and informing the public about the Notary's vital role in modern society. ■

Index

Page numbers listed in **bold** indicate where the most complete information on a subject can be found. *Italics* indicate pages where *The Notary Public Code of Professional Responsibility* addresses the subject.